Extraordinary Humans
The Early Years

An art-based approach and other very useful things

Hay Howell
A collaboration

For Liberty, Hamish and my parents.

This book is dedicated to every child that is or will be.

All children have the right to the best start in life.

We must be that child's champion, so they become the best they can possibly be.

We are not born equal, but, good teaching gives us the opportunity to develop each child's innate potential and instill the love of learning.

The future world is in our hands, the educators. We must light those fires.

…………

To Olivia, Alfie and Edgar who were lucky enough to begin their education as a Howell Hay collaboration.

Nicola Hay © Copyright 2021

The right of Nicola Hay to be identified as the author of this work has been asserted by her in accordance with the Copyright, Designs and Patents Act 1988.

All rights reserved.

No reproduction, copy or transmission of this publication may be made without express prior written permission. No paragraph of this publication may be reproduced, copied or transmitted except with express prior written permission or in accordance with the provisions of the Copyright Act 1956 (as amended). Any person who commits any unauthorised act in relation to this publication may be liable to criminal prosecution and civil claims for damage.

The author and publisher do not accept any responsibility for any loss, which may arise as a consequence of reliance on information contained in this book.

Illustrations: Joanna Howell
Photographer: Daisy Barnard Photography

Published by Goldcrest Books International Ltd
www.goldcrestbooks.com
publish@goldcrestbooks.com

ISBN: 978-1-911505-96-9
eISBN: 978-1-911505-97-6

Extraordinary Humans

About the author

Nicola Hay

Nicky has been teaching for over forty years. She has taught all primary ages, but most of her teaching has been in the Early Years.

For the last eight years of her teaching career she was head of The Foundation Stage and the teacher in charge of Bel Royal Primary School Nursery, Jersey. She is now delivering the WellComm language programme at Rouge Bouillon School, Jersey.

She is a passionate champion of the Early Years.

About the illustrator

Joanna Howell

Jo is a practicing artist and lectured at art college before having children and assisting Nicky at Bel Royal school nursery.

She tailored projects for Nicky's early years pupils from work that she did with degree level art students in sculpture, animation and printmaking.

Jo is an avid reader and collector of children's books.

MRS HAY

Contents

Why art?

Historical and pedagogical

What do we value in early childhood education?

What we believe

Cognitive development

Characteristics of effective learning

Creating and critical thinking

Learning and development – prime areas

Learning and development – specific areas

Developing social skills and collaboration

Self-regulation

Self-confidence and self-esteem

Well-being and motivation

State of flow

How did we start?

The adult facilitator

Staff

Adults engaged with children

How is learning measured?

Children as artists

Nursery organization

Skills

Our project

Displaying artwork

Other ideas, projects, and our belief in educating outdoors

Self-compassion

Equal opportunities

Health and safety

Special days

National days

Visitors to nursery

Visits

Fundraising

Real things

The nature table

Practical ideas

Outdoors

REAL and REAL maths

Final words

Appendix

Appendix 1   Beach School Handbook
Appendix 2   Forest School Handbook
Appendix 3   Risk assessment template
Appendix 4   Well-being and involvement
Appendix 5   Our favourite books for children
Appendix 6   Our top twenty favourite Illustrators
Appendix 7   Playdough
Appendix 8   Six steps to conflict resolutions
Appendix 9   A helpful quote

References

References

Select Bibliography

Useful websites

Introduction

1. Why art?

Art is a unique experience.

Art helps children to understand their world and make sense of their experiences. Art is a language; it allows us to express our emotions and develop ideas. Both sides of the brain are developed, increasing the capacity for memory, attention, and concentration.

Children are introduced to new concepts and vocabulary and in doing so develop their social skills with peers and adults.

Each experience a child has is a process; each discovery changing the child and pointing to fresh experiences and new investigations.

It is our responsibility to be a part of the child's learning experience, motivating them through meaningful dialogue. If we do not provide this interaction with art, then it becomes limited to only sensory experiences. A child adjusts their inner world of imagery to the outer world.

As practitioners we need to be able to see the difference between easily obtained, superficial outcomes and deep level learning.

> *An eye that sees, a hand that obeys, and a soul that feels.*
>
> Dr Montessori

We must remember that art is wide-reaching covering music, poetry, woodwork, textiles; it is using the human eye to give shape to something. Art is the representation and the science, the explanation of the same reality.

We have all seen the teacher-directed activity, the finished product already envisioned, pre-cut materials with steps for the children to follow.

Where has this come from?

- Wanting parents to recognize art.
- Lack of teacher confidence.
- The need for structure.

From these activities both the teacher and child gain nothing, there is no exploration; these activities will have a negative effect on the child, harming artistic confidence and development.

Skill acquisition should be embedded in meaningful experience.

> *Only when teacher stayed with a child and became involved in a dialogue related to actions that the child was performing, did the child seem inclined to truly explore the available materials and tools, or to experiment with their use.*
>
> Kindler (1997)

This book is our journey of growth through art.

We provided the children with a unique experience of learning through art. It will show how we achieved this, and the impact it had upon the children's self-esteem and confidence. How, with guidance, children mastered new skills and accomplished tasks that they initially perceived as unachievable.

2. History

We have used art as a tool to teach the children skills. This does not mean the children were not at other times given the freedom to use art as purely self-expression.

> *To learn a thing in life and through doing is much more developing, cultivating and strengthening than to learn it merely through the verbal communication of ideas.*
> Friedrich Froebel (1782–1852)

Friedrich Fröbel and other pioneers

Friedrich Fröbel (1782–1852) founded the Kindergarten movement. He saw children as holistic learners who learnt most effectively through action, whether it was using their hands or minds. He believed children should be involved in both making their own art and enjoying the art of others. To Fröbel, art activities were important, not because they allowed teachers to recognize children with unusual abilities, but because they encouraged each child's full and all-sided development.

Jean Piaget (1896–1980) emphasized active learning and the importance of cultivating the experimental mind.

The Reggio Emilia approach to early childhood education views young children as individuals who are curious about their world and have the powerful potential to learn from all that surrounds them. Educational, psychological, and sociological influences are important factors to consider in understanding children and working to stimulate learning in appropriate ways. Reggio teachers employ strategies such as exposing children to a wide variety of educational opportunities that encourage self-expression, communication, logical thinking, and problem-solving.

Reggio acknowledges art as a language and recognizes children's use of artist media as integral to the cognitive and symbolic expression involved in learning.

> *Early art exposure is critical and if unnurtured it may be difficult to recover.*
> Eisner (1998)

Many theories, Fowler (1989), Kindler (1997), Piscitelli (1993) and Wright (1991), all identified a gap in the teaching of art in the early years and suggests that teachers' lack of expertise contributes to this.

By nurturing children's talents and empowering them to be independent learners we can cultivate confidence, passion, and higher self-esteem. If we develop creative and critical thinking skills, curiosity, and interest we can foster a passion for lifelong learning.

There are questions to be asked:

- Where is art in your daily plans?
- What continuous provision is made for this?
- What professional development is being provided?

3. What we value

First and foremost, we value the unique child. It is the most important truth that learning starts here.

All teaching should nurture, engage, and motivate. Promoting in the child a sense of achievement and commitment to learning.

The following are vital for high quality excellence in education:

- Creativity and critical thinking: Being imaginative, understanding the need for quality in work.

- Respect: Adults and children are considerate, courteous, promoting positive self-belief and being team players.

- Compassion: Adults and children show a sense of empathy, recognizing the talents and strengths of others.

- Independence: Children source resources for themselves, help others, are thoughtful, reliable, and show the ability to lead and encourage others.

- Perseverance: Having a positive, persistent, effort and determination.

4. What we believe

All areas of the Early Years curriculum can be taught through art by providing the children with a holistic approach. Because art is a sensory, exploration activity, children build a knowledge of the world around them. Through art activities, they can learn to make decisions and conduct self-evaluations. Drawing helps them symbolize what they know and feel.

Gross and fine motor skills are developed and with repeated opportunities for practice, young children gain confidence in their use of tools for making art and later for writing.

> *Art also helps hand-eye coordination, as children decide how to make parts fit together as a whole, where to place objects, and what details to include, they learn to coordinate what they see with the movements of their hands and fingers.*
>
> Koster 1997

Hand-eye coordination is essential for many things, including forming letters, and spacing words in formal writing.

We know the importance Early Years Foundation Stage Development Matters puts upon the following, and we totally agree:

A unique child

+

positive relationships

+

enabling environments

=

Learning and development

> *Play is the highest expression of human development in childhood for it alone is the free expression of the child's soul.*
>
> Froebel (1826).

5. Cognitive development

The cognitive developments we are aiming to assist through art are; problem solving skills, observing cause and effect, and experimenting with unfamiliar and new materials.

Decision making is constant and continuous through projects. Children also learn about spatial relations and visual thinking skills.

Active learning & Playing and exploring

Children can explore with art, playing with possibilities. They are naturally curious and will investigate.

Play is the practice for real-life experience.

Children can explore through art, play with possibilities, and investigate new curiosities.

> *They will become more willing to embrace new experiences and less fearful when they are given the correct support and encouragement.*
>
> van Kuyk (2011).

Vygotsky (1978), spoke of the zone of proximal development, as children increase what they are able to do without the help of an adult. Children progressed from being supported to learning new skills and solve problems, they moved on to working unaided, extending, and building on their knowledge and learning, extending what he called their zone of proximal development. What a child can do with adult support today they will be able to do for themselves tomorrow. Children must be provided with opportunities to experiment and explore independently.

Art stimulates both sides of the brain and increases the capacity of memory, attention, and concentration. Therefore, children are more open to new vocabulary and making connections between concepts.

Art education should be exciting, relaxing, and enjoyable. Children need to be able to grow, develop, and learn in their artistic potential.

6. Characteristics of effective learning

Art can be seen to embrace all the characteristics of effective learning, through the exploration and investigation of materials and learning through first-hand experiences by using tools, with guided participation and scaffolding from the adult, and being creative. These factors are essential to ensure children develop and maintain an effective style of learning.

Playing and exploring – engagement

Finding out and exploring

- Showing curiosity about objects, events, and people.
- Using senses to explore the world around them.
- Engaging in open ended activity.
- Showing particular interest.

Playing with what they know

- Representing their experiences.
- Pretending objects are things from their experience.

Being willing to have a go
- Initiating activities.
- Seeking challenge.
- Showing a can-do attitude.
- Taking a risk, engaging in new experiences, and learning by trial and error.

Active Learning – motivation
Being involved and concentrating
- Maintaining focus on their activity for a long time.
- Showing high levels of energy, fascination.
- Not easily distracted.
- Pay attention to detail.

Keeping on trying
- Persisting with activity when challenges occur.
- Showing a belief that more effort or a different approach will pay off.
- Bouncing back after difficulties.

Enjoying achieving what they set out to do
- Showing satisfaction in meeting their own goals.
- Being proud of how they accomplished something – not just the end result.
- Enjoying meeting challenges for their own sake rather than external reward.

7. Creating and critical thinking

Having their own ideas

- Thinking of ideas.
- Finding ways to solve problems.
- Finding new ways to do things.

Making Links

- Making links and noticing patterns in their experience.
- Making predictions.
- Testing their ideas.
- Developing ideas of grouping, sequences, cause, and effect.

Choosing ways to do things

- Planning, making decisions about how to approach a task, solve a problem and reach a goal.
- Checking how well their activities are going.
- Changing strategy as needed.
- Reviewing how well the approach worked.

8. Learning and development – prime areas

Personal, social and emotional development

Children play co-operatively; taking turns with others by doing this they take account of one another's ideas about how to organize their activity. They show sensitivity to others' needs and feelings and form positive relationships with adults and fellow children.

Children are confident to try new activities and say why they like some activities more than others. They are happy to speak in a familiar group, will talk about their ideas, and will choose the resources they need for their chosen activities. Saying when they do or do not need help.

Communication and Language

- Children listen to others on a one to one, or in small groups, when the conversation interests them.
- Can focus attention.
- Are able to follow directions.
- They understand the use of objects.
- They respond to simple instructions.
- Use talk to connect ideas.
- Question why things happen and give explanations.
- Build up their vocabulary.

Physical Development

As children's fine and gross motor skills are developed, they learn a sense of awareness of the world around them.

Children show good control and coordination in large and small movements. They handle equipment and tools effectively.

9. Learning and development – specific areas

Literacy

- Children show an interest in illustrations and print in books and print in the environment.
- Sometimes give meanings to marks as they draw and paint.

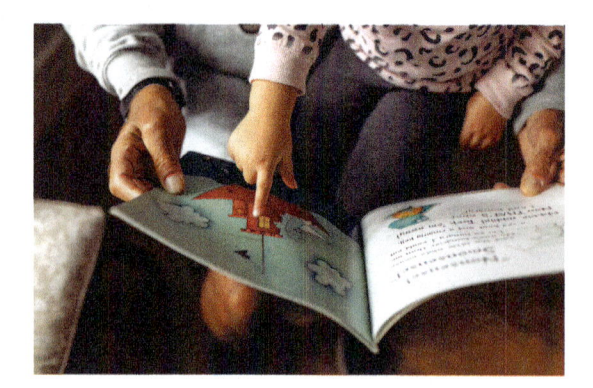

Maths

- Show an interest in shape and space.
- Show an awareness of similarities of shapes in the environment.
- Use positional language.
- Begin to talk about the shape of everyday objects, e.g. round and tall.

Understanding the world

- Know some of the things that make them unique.
- Can talk about some of the things they have observed.
- Know how to operate simple equipment.
- Know information can be retrieved from computers.
- Uses ICT hardware to interact with age appropriate software.

Expressive arts and design

They safely use and explore a variety of materials, tools, and techniques, experimenting with colour, design, texture, form, and function.

Children use what they have learnt about media and materials in original ways by thinking about the uses and purposes. They can represent their own ideas, thoughts, and feelings through art.

It must be remembered that all children develop at their own rate.

10. Developing social skills and collaboration

A very high priority in the Early Years must be given to developing social skills.

The skill of the adult is to create a culture where everyone wants to contribute their ideas, this means a nurturing, caring, and trusting environment has to be created. The adult needs to distinguish the differing needs of the learners. Giving reassurance and creating a safe place where everyone is valued and loved.

The key is remembering that play is practice for real life.

There are five basic areas of consideration when thinking about the development of social skills.

Expressing emotions: Children need to learn to put a name to what they are feeling. They need to verbalize how they are feeling, without throwing things or hitting others.

Communication: This is the importance of eye contact. Knowing and remembering to use the social conventions of please, thank-you and sorry.

Positive role models: Older children, peers and adults can all be positive role models. Children have to learn the difference between being polite and rude.

Listening: Children will need to be taught the importance of listening and turn-taking.

Group work: Through group work, children will begin to understand socialization. They will realize the importance of non-verbal skills by reading facial expressions, and by learning body language cues. Through this they can learn how to deal with conflict to talk constructively.

11. Self-regulation

What is it and why is it important?

Self-regulation is about managing thoughts and feelings to enable children to socialize with others and achieve their goals.

A child with good self-regulation displays the following characteristics:

- Listens.
- Can focus and shift attention.
- Cooperates with others and can take turns.
- Asks for help.
- Acts responsibly.
- Shows kindness.
- Controls their temper in conflict.
- Follows directions and rules.

How does self-regulation develop?

It is like all other skills and can be taught. To learn self-regulation adults should support children through scaffolding when they feel challenged.

Adults must model self-control and self-regulation in words and actions.

Keep a structured and predictable routine. Children that display problems with self-regulation are internally unstructured. They may have little or no structure in their home life.

Keep the colours in the environment neutral. Make the environment calmer with areas for quiet play. Keep the general noise levels low. Allow children plenty of exercise and outdoor play.

There must be a timetable time for relaxation and yoga.

> *Without security as a background to his life he cannot dare to explore or experiment, to express his feelings or to try out new relations to people.*
> Isaac (1952).

12. Self-confidence and self-esteem

A child's confidence and independence will grow as they master new skills and techniques.

A child's self-esteem is helped with gentle guidance from the adult. Reassurance, acknowledgement that the child has tackled challenges, overcoming obstacles and honest praise are key to building positive self-esteem.

Fostering a growth mindset, learning from mistakes and being supportive but realistic are all key to helping a child develop positive self-esteem. Carol Dweck (2006) talks about fixed and growth mindsets:

> *"A growth mindset tolerates challenge, risk, failure and sets children up to be life-long learners."*

13. Well-being and motivation

To motivate is to provoke or incite interest.

Art provides multi-sensory motivation; exploratory experience of art materials can be incredibly motivating.

Emotional well-being

Ferre Laevers

Ferre is the director of the research centre for experimental education based at the University of Leuven, Belgium.

He sees a child's well-being and the intensity of his or her mental activity (involvement) as key for the power of the learning environment and a condition for "deep level learning".

The work of Ferre Laevers highlights the importance of well-being and involvement.

Well-being

A child with high well-being feels at ease and acts spontaneously. They are open to the world and are accessible. The child will express inner rest and relaxation. They will show vitality and radiate.

Involvement

Children will display interest, be motivated and fascinated. They will be mentally active, fully experiencing sensations and meanings.

They will be enjoying the satisfaction of the exploratory drive. They will be operating at the very limits of their capabilities.

Because of this we know that deep level learning will be taking place.

14. State of flow

Mihaly Csikszentmihalyi (1990) talks about flow and being in a state of flow. A state of flow produces a feeling of happiness and inner fulfilment, "in an activity nothing else seems to matter; the experience is so enjoyable that people will continue to do it even at great cost, for the sheer sake of doing it". He states that flow was most likely to occur in situations combining high skills with a high level of challenge.

15. How did we start?

A Nursery is the most interesting place on earth. It represents all that is human, the past, the present and the future. It is always about understanding the holistic quality of teaching and learning. A child is never a sole entity. They come with a past, however short, with carers or family and extended family. Their previous learning is diverse and so is their individual experience of life. Home backgrounds are never equal. Some of these extraordinary humans have never had to share, or mix, with other children or adults before.

The gap between a child entering and leaving the school nursery setting is the largest in the whole primary school.

We must acknowledge this and find a mutually acceptable baseline to start. This will vary each year as every cohort of children is different. Sometimes, certain personalities make for a difficult year, where your priorities have to be different.

16. The adult facilitator

All adults must have high expectations of the child. They must all understand the importance of the art experience for the child.

Adults must be flexible and tolerant, letting the child flourish. Adults should model, scaffold and work alongside the child. It is all about balance and being responsive to the child. Adults must allow the child to move out of their comfort zone, letting them take risks, raising questions and challenges. The skill of the adult is to create a safe environment, where everyone wants to contribute their ideas.

> *Each time one prematurely teaches a child something he could have discovered himself, that child is kept from inventing it and consequently from understanding it completely.*
>
> Piaget (1959).

In a nursery you must embrace the chaos. It is not easy to do this. Having a few of the following qualities is a prerequisite:

- Be a listener.
- Dedicated.
- Compassionate.
- Organized.
- Creative and enthusiastic.
- A team player.
- Involved.
- A reader of people. Show empathy. Know which outside agencies are available to help families with their problems.
- Keep up to date with research; be a learner yourself.
- A risk taker.

In fact, possess all the qualities we try to instill in our children.

It is vital that the planning, staff, and equipment are at the very highest standard you can achieve. This can't happen overnight, but a serious development plan is necessary with realistic targets.

17. Staff

Most of us are not lucky enough to choose our own staff. There may be restrictions on funds, and you may feel that you are understaffed. So, it is very important to train the children to become independent and follow the nursery routines from day one.

However, you must take your staff along with any of your plans. Listen to their ideas and use their strengths.

Staff training is vital. External training and in-house, both provide impact. Mentoring and broadening knowledge means all staff have a better understanding of children, their needs, parents, how children learn and the way forward.

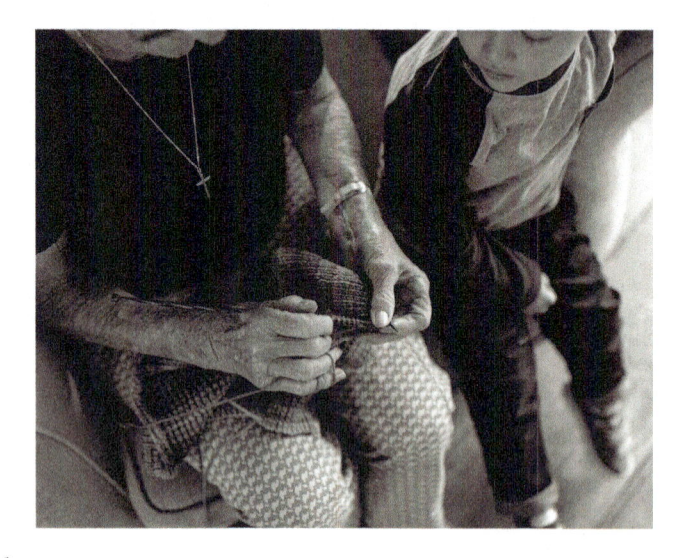

The way we talk to children, role model and interact are fundamental to all practice.

Interactions

Teaching happens through interactions. These are the sorts of interactions we should see between adults and children:

- Allowing time
- Following child's interest
- Encouraging
- Modelling behaviour, language and skills
- Demonstrating
- Suggesting
- Scaffolding
- Observing
- Listening

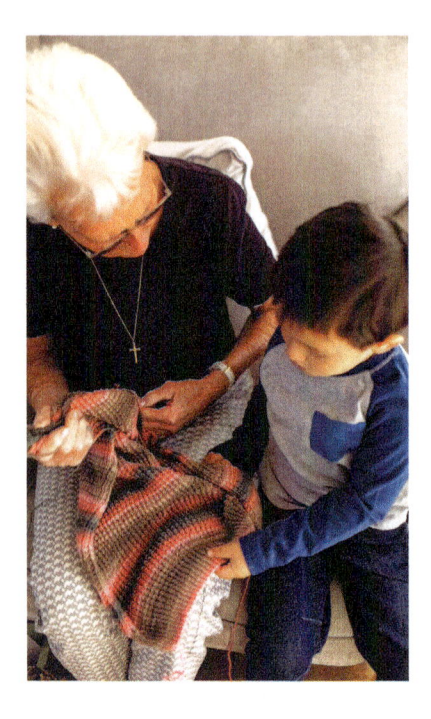

18. Adults engaged with children would be:

- Happy
- Relaxed
- At child's level
- Calm
- Interacting
- Positive
- Quiet
- Confident
- Listening

Children are engaged, we would see:

- Busy
- Happy
- Comfortable
- Secure
- Purposeful
- Chatting
- Socializing
- Independent
- Self-motivated
- Confident
- Risk taking

19. How is learning measured?

We must remember that not all learning is measurable by ticking off early learning goals, but by children's engagement, well-being, and motivation, and also by parents' feelings towards the setting and their child's happiness and development.

> *Individual learning, flexibility in the curriculum, the centrality of play in children's learning, the use of the environment, learning by discovery and the importance of the evaluation of children's progress-teachers should not assume that only what is measurable is valuable.*
> Piaget (1957).

There are many opportunities in art to observe and monitor progress. This includes staff discussions and reflections.

> *Our task regarding creativity, is to help children climb their own mountains, as high as possible. No one can do more.*
> Loris Malaguzzi (1920–1994)

20. Children as artists

It is never about control.

If you believe this, you're in the wrong job.

All kinds of materials are used by children to show what they have noticed about their world.

What conditions do children need to become artists?
- Being out in all weathers.
- Dancing and singing in the rain, tasting rain drops.
- Collecting leaves, playing with mud.
- Listening to music.
- Going to the beach.
- Making a campfire.
- Smelling plants.
- Lying looking at the sky.
- Cooking.
- Listening to sounds.
- Using all their senses – touching, smelling, listening, hearing, and seeing.

21. Nursery organization

A nursery should only show child-generated mess each day, all adult clutter is cleared away and not left on display. Continuous provision should have open-ended resources that encourage creative and critical thinking as well as imagination. With effective provision we must consider basic provision, continuous provision, and enhanced provision.

The atmosphere must be relaxed with many conversations and pleasant social interactions. It is important for staff and children to feel at home in a setting.

The flexible environment, with room for initiative, must give children the freedom of movement, as child senses can only be educated in action.

A balance between a home and a workshop atmosphere is ideal, with thought to lighting, wall colours and fresh flowers.

Hygiene is very important. Children must be taught about germs and the importance of self-care, handwashing, toileting and nose blowing.

An enriched environment can offer the children opportunities to explore reality.

Invitations to learn

We used crates to display themed topics. We would have a selection of these around the Nursery to introduce the children to new ideas or revisit old themes.

For example, traditional tales – large Red Riding Hood and wolf puppets, with the picnic basket and contents, and the story book.

Sea shells with a non-fiction book. A bucket with sea creatures and the book Billy's Bucket, by Kes Gray, one of our favourites.

Art area

Maintenance and organization are key.

This needs to be well-stocked. All stock needs to be replenished regularly and equipment kept clean and in good condition.

It is important that resources are accessible, as children will need to use these independently. There should be a creative space inside and outside as part of your continuous provision, e.g. a sandpit is a great place for sand sculptures.

Brushes, crayons and markers – Brushes, crayons, and markers are important materials to have in any art area. Remember to have brushes, crayons pens and pencils of different sizes.

Chalk – Take art activities outside with fun chalk materials or use chalk on chalkboards indoors.

Clay, dough and modelling materials – Children will have fun using their hands to make creative statues and models with dough and modelling clay. Use rolling pins, cutters, beads, etc.

Collage and craft materials – Offer a variety of art supplies for any collage or craft projects, including craft sticks, feathers, pipe cleaners, wool, boxes, tubes, etc.

Glue, tape and adhesives – Help children keep their project together, add hole punchers, treasury tags, tape, glue, and other adhesives.

Paint and paint materials – Stock your art area with a variety of paints including finger paint and watercolour paint, among others. Sponges, paint pots, and paint markers are also necessary.

Paper and scissors – Stimulate children's senses by giving them the chance to use paper in different textures, colours, and sizes – newspaper, rolls of paper, tracing paper, scrap paper, bubble wrap, cereal boxes, leaves, tissue paper.

Inks and ink pads – Children love to use inks, especially if they have been involved in making their own.

Natural materials – Leaves, sticks, feathers, petals, sand, mud, and pebbles.

Equipment must be kept to the highest standard and replaced when necessary.

I would not be tempted to use equipment that was dirty, or in a poor state of repair, so why should children be treated any differently?

Even in state-funded nurseries it is important to raise your own money to provide for the extras you always need. (Please see Chapter 38 for fundraising ideas.)

22. Skills

Children must be taught certain skills before they can independently work on tasks:

- Gluing.
- Using scissors.
- Mixing paints.
- Squeeze/roll and join clay.
- How to make patterns.
- Using paint brushes.

For each area of the curriculum, it is necessary to give all staff a clear idea of the progression of skills.

For example:

Area ...Printing

HIGH	Different shapes, brushes, car wheels, lino prints.
MEDIUM	Sponges.
LOW	Hands.

23. Our project

Language

Originally our project spiralled out of a need to deliver a language programme.

We were using WellComm, a complete speech and language toolkit to both screen the children and plan for their development. WellComm helped us to identify areas of language we needed to work on; we wove this targeted language into each of our projects.

Activities

REAL body drawing

An amazing activity for gross motor development and for social skills. Your friend draws around your body on a very large roll of paper. The rest is up to the individual child. They can embellish their outline, however they wish. This gives you a fabulous insight into how each child sees themselves.

Story pebbles

In the nursery we know children will need, sooner or later, to translate their creativity into the written word. With this in mind we were always story scribers for the children. This enables children to discover the world around them in their own way, a very personal way. These stories were illustrated by the children and made into books.

We decorated a range of beach pebbles to use as visual prompts to start the children talking and use their imaginations.

A story has five basic but important elements. These are characters, settings, plot, the conflict, and the resolution.

The pebbles contained all five of these areas.

The pebbles were particularly helpful with reluctant talkers.

Helicopter stories followed on from the pebbles.

(Princesses, Dragons and Helicopter Stories: Storytelling and story acting in the early years by Trisha Lee).

Own ink drawings each term

Each term the children would do a self-portrait with ink. These would be displayed together to help the parents see their child's development and progression throughout the year.

This activity was essential for teaching language of body parts and uses of body parts.

When you are working alongside a child, have your own piece of paper to demonstrate. NEVER be tempted to add to a child's work.

Own portraits

This activity was a development from our ink drawings. The children just concentrated on their faces. Mirrors were used and this involved great discussions. Hair colour and skin colour are great starting points and useful for teaching colour mixing.

Making charcoal and observational drawings

We made our own charcoal over the open fire during one of our Forest School sessions. This we used to make all different kinds of observational drawings.

Hand lenses are a great tool for this activity.

Nature portraits

The children's nature portraits were a natural follow-on from our self-portraits. We took this activity outside and the children were allowed to decide what materials from the garden they would use. This included mud, sand, twigs, moss, leaves, berries, etc.

The children mixed mud and sand with lots of PVA. They painted with this mixture and then the leaves, berries, etc. could stick to it easily.

Recycling building

This has a lovely name – JUNKLING – as named by Scoot.

We were lucky enough to have space to store good quality junk. This was carefully stored and sorted. The children had access to it and could use it when they liked. However, our building project was on a one to one and scaffolded by the adult. This meant language weaving could take place.

All skills leading up to this activity were taught prior to the activity itself, such as joining boxes together, handling glue, and cutting skills.

We followed these steps to deliver this activity:

The children wanted to make robots, so we talked about their emotions and facial expressions.

- We used photographs of faces to prompt the discussion.
- Children were reminded of joining techniques.

The children were shown how they could make different parts move. For example, the tongue moved in and out.

All the different techniques taught were tailored to the individual needs of the children and their ideas for their project.

Animation

Once our self-portraits were completed, we used them together to make a special animated film. The children were all involved in the production of this. It was used as our special movie to show the parents and grandparents at the end of term.

The process developed in the following steps:

- We cut out their portraits.
- We made a storyboard.
- The children used this to position arms and heads and used it for reference.
- We set up a tripod with steps. The children each framed their photographs and then took it.
- Each child uploaded their photograph to the app. Stop Motion.
- Each child was shown how to load their images in sequence then press play.

We even had a clapper board and the shout of "Action" was heard repeatedly across the nursery.

Mark making

Mark making is any mark made using any material on any surface, such as:

- pencil on paper
- scratch in clay
- paint on a canvas

A mark can be a line, a dot, a scratch, a curve, a thumbprint and so on. Using different tools can help create different thicknesses and types of marks.

Ink making

Make Ink: A Forager's Guide to Natural Inkmaking by Jason Logan was our great resource. We made numerous different kinds of inks; some were more successful than others.

Making the ink was a long process, the copper pipe ink was particularly successful. It had to sit on the windowsill for a while. This produced a great deal of questioning and chatter from the children as they independently went back to look at the inks.

The children enjoyed making the inks and subsequently, they had more ownership when using them.

Small fairy pens and giant pens were made. We used sticks, brushes, and feathers to make marks with our ink.

This is a great activity for reluctant mark makers, especially if the mark making activity takes place outside.

Printing

We tried monoprinting with the children. This again was a success and the children quickly learnt the terminology and the techniques.

Monoprinting is the process of making a print using 'mark making'.

A monoprint is a one-of-a-kind print. Every single print you take with this process is unique. You can place a second piece of paper onto the painted surface to take a second print and compare how it is different from the first. The paint is also really easy to wipe or wash off, so you can enjoy all the sensory delights of adding more paints and creating a whole series of monoprints.

Steps to monoprinting:

- The colour used to create monoprints is usually water-based ink. A roller is used to apply the ink evenly over the printing plate.

- You start by making paint patterns on a piece of Plexiglas. You can use brushes, or fingers, and even squirt the paint straight onto the Plexiglas. It's a really sensory process.

- Carefully place a piece of paper or card over your paint.

- Then using a roller press down on the paper.

- Carefully peel back your paper to reveal your monoprint.

- More than one print can be made each time.

24. Displaying artwork

Nursery children in particular find it hard to leave their work in their setting and not take it home.

Therefore, adults should be sensitive to this and some work that is their own should go home immediately. However, it should be explained to the children that selected art pieces might need to be displayed in the nursery for a while before being taken home.

Decisions about the display of their work need to be made in discussion with the child artist. We must acknowledge children's rights in relationship to the child as an artist.

Sensitivity and respect with children's artwork is crucial to self-esteem and interest in art.

Negotiation with the child gives them respect and supports their rights. Discussing their artwork with the child is very powerful.

Display needs to be selective, don't overwhelm. As in gardening, odd numbers are the key. Group display pictures or photographs in odd numbers.

We found that displaying artwork needed a neutral background such as plain hessian. A plain ribbon edge helps to keep a professional look.

Most settings have difficulty with display; often boards are too few or too many. They can be too high or too low.

We were not against writing quotes in paint on our walls.

> Margaret McMillan's quote was one of our favourites:
> *"The best store cupboard and classroom is roofed only by the sky."*

25. Other ideas, projects, and our belief in educating outdoors

Sewing

We were so very lucky to have Mrs Sewing Clarke, who came into the nursery weekly, to sew with the children on an individual basis.

- Sewing offers an enormous amount of benefits:
- Practise communication and following instructions.
- Imagination/creativity.
- Self-confidence/patience.
- Perseverance.
- Self-esteem.
- Concentration/focus.
- Development of hand-eye co-ordination, and fine motor skills.
- Fostering a sense of accomplishment.

Mrs Sewing Clarke, although well-past retirement age, worked tirelessly, so all the children could produce work for the Eisteddfod each year.

The work on display was visited by whole families, developing a shared sense of pride between the child and their family.

Relaxation and yoga activities

We found that both yoga and mindfulness helped to improve the physical and mental health of the children. Without doubt, yoga improves balance, strength, endurance and aerobic capacity. Yoga and mindfulness have psychological benefits too.

Yoga can improve focus, memory, self-esteem, academic performance, as well as reducing anxiety and stress.

It is great fun for adults in the classroom, as well as the children.

There are an enormous amount of resources on the internet to use for both yoga and mindfulness.

I preferred to deliver my own lessons, as I am a big yoga fan. I found A4 sized photographs of either the animals for the animal poses, or photographs of the children holding various poses, were useful aide-mémoires for the children.

Useful resources

- Cosmic Kids yoga, online.
- Cosmic Kids, app.
- Yoga for kids with Alissa Kepas, online.
- www.yogajournal.com has all the yoga poses for children.
- www.kidsyogastories.com have free printable resources.

Staff well-being

Staff well-being is key to a happy and safe working environment.

I initiated a Pilates and meditation class after work, once a week for the staff.

This was a great success and helped bond the team together.

26. Self-compassion

98% of our thoughts we had yesterday, we have today. This is not good if they were negative.

- Motivating young children and young people through the cultivation of self-compassion.
- Understand the meaning of self-compassion.
- To recognize the benefits of self-compassion and how it relates to motivation.
- To consider self-compassion for ourselves and how this benefits those around us.
- To learn some exercises that can be undertaken by children to help cultivate greater self-compassion.
- Kristin Neff's model of self-compassion:

MINDFULNESS + COMMON HUMANITY + KINDNESS

Mindfulness - paying attention to the present moment on purpose and in a particular way.

Common humanity - recognition that suffering is part of the human condition. We are connected by our struggles rather than being isolated.

Kindness - treating myself with the same kindness as I would treat a friend who was struggling.

Backdraft

This is something that might happen when you are thinking about kindness.

- Thinking about kindness brings to mind the opposite. We know what light is because of the dark – hot/cold.

Grounding

This needs to be a drip effect. Slowly, be kind to yourself.

Four helpful techniques:

- Butterfly hug – start with fingers tap, tap, tap, like a heartbeat. Magic dust.
- Be aware of your feet pushing down – barefoot.
- 54321 – 5 see, 4 hear, 3 touch, 2 taste, 1 smell.
- You might need a stone to keep in your pocket.

Soothing touch – the power of touch.

- Keep contact warm, and soft verbalization. These release feel-good oxytocin.
- Put hand on heart ... with inner talk ... I'll be O.K. Tone of voice.

Benefits of self-compassion are strongly associated with:

- Emotional well-being.
- Improved mood.
- Less anxiety and stress.
- Maintenance of healthy habits such as diet and exercise.
- Satisfying personal relationships.
- Reduced caregiver fatigue.

What prevents us from being more compassionate?

Some misgivings are:

- It's self-pity.
- It is self-indulgent.
- It is weak.
- It is selfish.
- It is making excuses.
- It undermines motivation.

Volition-Kielhofner's model

The cognitive process by which an individual decides on and commits to a particular course of action.

Volition depends upon:

Interests

Values – these are very important in terms of motivation.

Personal causation – how able they think they are to do this? One's sense of competence and effectiveness. (Lots of shut down in the classroom. Fear of failure.)

A moment for me

- Use mindful meditation but apply it to ourselves first. Follow the model of self-compassion.

Self-compassion versus self-criticism

Self-compassion is about self-acceptance. It is not about self-improvement. *ACCEPT WHO YOU ARE AS YOU ARE.*

We all have the tendency to believe self-doubt and self-criticism but listening to this voice never gets us closer to our goals. Instead, try on the point of view of a mentor or good friend who believes in you, wants the best for you and will encourage you when you feel discouraged.

Kelly McGonigal (2011), psychologist and author.

Motivating with self-compassion exercise.

What is the behaviour or problem?

1. Stop thinking about the next steps – do something about them.

2. How does this present itself? Are you going around in circles? Your self-critical voice. What is the problem?

3. How does the inner critic behave itself – word/tone of voice, facing a wall, sense of ending, not moving forward, waiting?

4. How does it feel to be on the end of the critical voice? Does it impact in any way?

5. Take a sympathetic moment for yourself. Acknowledge this is difficult, this hurts. What motivates the inner voice?

6. Reflect – why have this voice? Was the voice the voice of the care giver in the past?

7. Is the inner critic trying to protect you? Trying to help you move on?

8. Need to thank the inner critic for supporting you – might not be helping but the intention was good.

Compassionate voice

This wants you to change ... reflect on who you are ... it wants the best for you ... I love you? I don't want you to suffer. I deeply care for you. I'm here to support you.

Write a letter to yourself – what would you say to you right now?

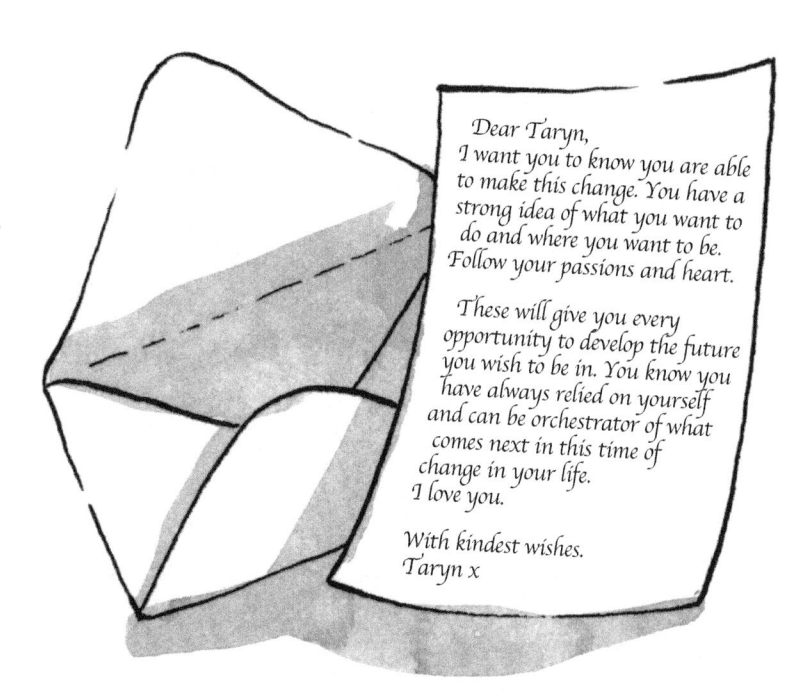

Dear Taryn,

I want you to know you are able to make this change. You have a strong idea of what you want to do and where you want to be. Follow your passions and heart.

These will give you every opportunity to develop the future you wish to be in. You know you have always relied on yourself and can be orchestrator of what comes next in this time of change in your life.
I love you.

With kindest wishes.
Taryn x

Giving and receiving compassion

For someone to develop genuine compassion towards others, first he or she must have a basis upon which to cultivate compassion, and that basis is the ability to connect to one's own feelings and to care for one's own welfare.

Caring for others requires caring for oneself.

Tips for encouraging self-compassion in children and young people:

- Develop your own self-compassion, not only will this help improve awareness, empathy, and well-being, but it will also give authenticity.
- Model self-compassionate talk and behaviour.
- Validate emotional expression and promote the sense of connection with others (common humanity) rather than disconnection.
- Teach grounding practices, such as soles of the feet or 54321.
- Introduce soothing touch.
- Use kind communication and keep any criticism focused on the behaviour and not the person. Design feedback that is supportive and encouraging.
- A moment for me meditation.
- If a child is being harshly self-critical, ask, how would you treat a friend who is going through the same as you.
- Be aware of the emotional needs of the child, such as seen, heard, understood and to belong.
- Practise giving and receiving compassion when connecting with a child who is struggling.

Time to reflect

Meditation, sounds, feelings, touch.

> *"The curious paradox is that when I accept myself as I am, I can change."*
> Carl Rogers.

27. Equal opportunities

> *Art breaks through barriers that divide human beings, which are impermeable in ordinary association.*
> Dewey, 1934.

All children have the right to equal opportunities.

Research has shown that gaps between children's knowledge and experiences can be closed when high quality support is provided in the early years. Children's life chances are enhanced by quality early education and home learning environment. The EPPE project (Effective Provision Pre-school Education, 2004) found effective pedagogy includes structured interactions between staff and children. The provision of instructive learning environments and sustained shared thinking to extend children's learning.

- Early life experiences will impact on a child.
- The following must be considered when planning to close the educational gap:
- Fewer first-hand experiences.
- Lower levels of language (EAL).
- Lower levels of concentration.
- Lower levels of self-esteem/self-confidence.

All of these will impact on curiosity, resilience, and empathy. It is vital to find the child's starting point to readdress disadvantage.

There should be no gender difference or disadvantage for children with Special Educational Needs.

When planning, each child must be thought of as an individual. It must be remembered when planning sensory experiences that constant re-evaluation is needed to see what is working. Refinements and improvements can be made constantly to ensure inclusivity and provide targeted development.

28. Health and safety

> *If you are going to keep children safe, you must provide places in which they can get the thrills they need; there must be trees they can climb and ways in which they can safely get the experience and sense of challenge that they crave.*
> (Susan Issacs, 1937).

All of our projects have been low risk because they have been supervised correctly. But it is important to have an understanding of risk. Children need to understand risk and challenges too, meeting these in a safe environment.

Risk assessments are part of everyday life in nursery. They show the likelihood to harm or injury by a potential hazard. Please see a risk assessment in Appendix 3, if you need help compiling one.

29. Special days

Elf and Fairy Day

This was a favourite with the children. Everyone came into nursery wearing their outfits.

The day started with the children receiving a letter from Fairy Primrose.

I used a tooth fairy camera app. for the fairy to travel through the nursery and the nursery garden. We showed this to the children on the big screen. There were squeals of delight as they realized it was their nursery and garden.

> Bramble House
> Nettle Lane
> Fairyland
>
> Dear Children,
> I am writing to you in the hope that you can help me. There has been a big storm here in Fairyland and my garden has been ruined. Please could you help me to rebuild it? I am sending you a packet of special fairy dust to help transport you to Fairyland. Please use the fairy dust very carefully.
> I hope you can read my writing. I have tried to write VERY BIG.
> Lots of love from
> Fairy Primrose
> xxx

The children were transported to fairyland with the help of Fairy Primrose and fairy dust; they travelled through a time portal. We made an obstacle course to enter the nursery garden, remembering to leave enough space for wings.

The children were invited to use the resources to build a garden for Primrose.

There were plenty of other activities that were elf and fairy orientated, especially popular were the tiny books with tiny pens and ink.

We had a special picnic with tiny sandwiches and fairy named food and drinks.

The letters in reply to Fairy Primrose were endless.

Dads' morning

This was held in June, around Fathers' Day.

It is amazing what the allure of a bacon roll and a cuppa can do. The fathers were lured into the nursery, sharing a morning of activities with the children.

A great bonding morning between fathers and children and fathers and fathers. If it was impossible for the father to attend, we were more than happy to have another representative from the family.

Mums' morning

This was held in March, around Mothering Sunday. It was very much the same organization as the Fathers' day. We always learnt a song to perform too, when we all got together.

On both these occasions be prepared for tears when it's time for the parents to leave.

Mad Hatter's tea party

The Mad Hatter's tea party was an end of term event, held in the nursery garden.

Parents and grandparents were all invited. Everyone was welcome to dress up as a character from Alice in Wonderland and share a picnic lunch.

We had a special Alice in Wonderland cake made, which we all shared. The children were heavily involved in the organization of the lunch and afternoon events, preparing and decorating the garden. They made flower arrangements, signs, and character posters.

Garden party

This was a variation on the Mad Hatter's tea party, but we used this as a fundraiser. We made jams and chutneys with our home-grown produce and sold it on the day to parents and grandparents.

We also went to the local wholesaler and sold drinks, snacks and ice creams, for a small profit.

Movie morning

Each year we made a film for the parents. This was based around the year in nursery; a culmination of stills and small video clips. The children added voice-overs and it lasted roughly twenty minutes.

On two mornings we played the movie, once for parents and once for grandparents. This was accompanied by popcorn and a blacked-out nursery.

At the end of the year we burned the discs for the parents to buy.

This did, however, involve a confidentiality agreement between all parents.

Sports morning

We used our Sports morning to encourage the parents to play with their children. Each activity was based around a theme and parents were asked to have a go with their children.

At the end, they were all presented with a medal.

Buddy mornings with Year 6

We shared books on a weekly basis with our Year 6 buddies.

The Year 6 children were great role models for the younger children, and it was lovely to watch as the children bonded.

Once a term we held Buddy Mornings, we based these on mathematics. The older children were briefed on the activities, and also given instructions on the language to use to develop awareness in the younger children.

Buddy mornings lend themselves to all the different areas of the curriculum.

30. National Days

Make the most of National Days

Just look up National Days on the internet, there are certainly plenty.

Here are just a few we celebrated throughout the year.

They were great to introduce new ideas and themes and injecting fun into learning.

National Hat Day

Hats from around the world always came into the nursery, showing different sorts of cultures, occupations and pastimes.

My favourite was a swimming cap.

National Poetry Day

The children were encouraged to bring in their favourite poem they read at home.

We were lucky enough one year to have a poem written for us by a poet.

National Porridge Day

This lent itself nicely to Goldilocks and the Three Bears, and porridge tasting with various toppings.

National Squirrel Awareness Week

We were very fond of red squirrels, we had them inside and outside the nursery.

We had Cyril the Squirrel and his family, (knitted), who lived in the nursery. He was a generous squirrel and gave out golden acorns for acts of kindness. He kept a beady eye on the children.

We encouraged real red squirrels into our nursery garden by feeding them and with rope walks.

International Mud Day

The greatest of days. Mud is a sensory joy, and it's fun and free. Please do warn parents first, making sure each child has old clothes to change into.

Here are just a few things we tried: mud pies, cakes, painting, mark making, tree spirits, brick laying, soup, and body painting.

Day of Languages

We usually celebrated this in September, so that each child felt welcomed into the nursery. It is not always possible to celebrate all the languages spoken, however, it is worth a try. You might have to stretch this over a few weeks. With a little help and encouragement, most parents were willing to come into nursery and share stories or an activity, in their first language.

Global Handwashing Day

This has taken a new significance in the light of Covid-19. Children need to be taught this valuable skill. Once taught, they must be constantly reminded of how to do it.

Photographs and step-by-step visual guides should be on the wall by the children's sinks.

Pyjama Day

The children loved pyjama day, when they could put on their pyjamas and bring in a cuddly. Generally, this was book or story orientated, however, it proved so popular that the children often requested it. When they did this, we raised money for their chosen charity.

National Popcorn Day

This was a great fundraiser – we always sold popcorn to the rest of the school.

National Tree Dressing Day

A day for fabulous, creative fun outside. We always promoted hugging trees, so wrapping trees in ribbon, or decorating them with our created arts, was just a small sidestep.

World Nursery Rhyme Week

A great way to promote rhymes and remind parents of the benefits of sharing rhymes with their child.

World Kindness Day

This day gave a focus for the children to understand the meaning of kindness; a quality that is often neglected.

National Hug-a-Bear Day

Bears and bear stories feature a great deal in the Early Years. Over time we had collected a vast quantity of bears, so the children could hug them at story time, or read to a bear themselves.

National Storytelling Week

This is an opportunity to invite other people into your setting to read to the children or to tell a story. Parents, grandparents, authors, and staff members can all be asked to contribute.

Pancake Day

Who doesn't love a pancake? Maybe the person cooking the 100 pancakes! The batter can be made in advance with the children and a couple of precooked pancakes in a cool pan can be used to help the children toss them.

World Book Day

This really does depend on your school or setting. Some settings embrace the day with everyone dressing up, with authors and illustrators invited in.

If this doesn't happen in your setting then you can have as much excitement, but on a smaller scale. Set the example and then encourage others to join in.

Red Nose Day

A favourite charity day. We always sold red noses to the whole school. The children could take responsibility for the selling, and the Comic Relief website www.comicrelief.com has plenty of information and ideas.

Jersey Day

Living in Jersey we are lucky enough to have our own heritage to celebrate.

We made flags, tried Jersey Wonders, Black Butter and Cabbage Loaf. We invited in guest speakers, made flags, and learnt 'Beautiful Jersey'.

You could always pick, St George's, St David's, St Patrick's, or St Andrew's days. Or make up a day to celebrate your local heritage.

Healthy Eating Week

We held this during National Healthy Eating week, which is held every year. The website to go to is www.nutrition.org.uk where you can register and have access to wonderful resources, such as guides and posters.

Each day of the week would have a different focus. This was very much a home/school project and the parents were encouraged to participate.

- Eat more wholegrains.
- Vary your veg.
- Drink plenty.
- Move more.
- Be mind-kind.
- Get active together.
- Eat together.

Invite in guest speakers in for the week. Contact local organizations to support your Healthy Eating Week. For example, invite in a chef to show the parents how to produce healthier lunch boxes. Invite a fitness instructor to run a lunchtime class on your 'move more' day.

Aspiration Day

The children were again encouraged to dress up, this time as someone they aspired to be… fire fighters/chefs/librarians/storytellers.

The Pope came to nursery that day.

31. Visitors to the nursery

Here is a list, of just a few, different ideas of people that make a big difference by coming into your setting and working alongside the children. They are all kind enough to give of their time freely.

- Reading support
- Police
- Recycling team
- Vets
- Dentists
- Biodiversity
- Hedgehog sanctuary
- JSPCA/RSPCA
- Jersey Trees for Life or similar
- National Trust
- Older relatives and visitors

32. Visits

If your group is large it can be split into groups, we managed to use two minibuses for our trips that we couldn't walk to. As this had a high cost factor, we tried to keep to one minibus trip per half term.

Keep it simple – where can we walk to from here?

- Postbox
- Environmental print walk
- Number/shape walk
- Nature walk
- Beach
- Supermarket
- The park
- Train ride
- Catch the bus
- Laundrette
- Old Age home
- Scavenger hunt
- Cafe
- Using the minibus
- Library
- Woodland wander
- Rock pooling
- Bug safari
- The zoo
- Museum

33. Fundraising

All parents were asked to make a voluntary contribution each week of five pounds. This was primarily for snacks. However, we did manage to use this for cooking activities, play dough, and herbs and spices for potion mixes.

We had many ideas for fundraisers and managed to buy an enormous amount of equipment.

Companies are not willing to give money unless you are a registered charity, however, parents are good at persuading their companies to donate. So, bringing parents on board with plans is an excellent idea.

Fundraising ideas

Enter competitions. These are great. Look out in the local press and online for details. People are always eager to promote things and with a little effort these can be easy to win. They often provide vouchers or cash for prizes in return for publicity. Or the children receive prizes, again fabulous for promoting, home/nursery goodwill.

- The Eisteddfod. We always entered our sewing and cooking in the local Eisteddfod. This was very well-received by both the parents and children, especially when they gained their certificates, or the whole school retained the Mirehouse Shield.

- A sponsored Big Walk. This was always our biggest fundraiser of the year.

- A class cookbook – parents and staff all contribute ideas. This is a great multicultural and diverse way of bringing together the families. Easy to collate and either print out or use as a digital copy.

- Make play dough, put in jars, and add cutters.

- Grow and sell your own vegetables.

- Make and sell your own chutneys and jams.

- Sell tickets to showcase work, e.g. art gallery or home movie.

- Cake sale/fruit sale/popcorn sale.

- Summer Fair. A whole family affair with stalls selling homemade goods and various gifts for the children, e.g. bubbles, buckets and spades, ice-creams, balls, and drinks.

- Car wash.

- Toy/book sale.

Saving Money

We always, where possible, tried to save money on things.

- Buying spices, flour, etc. in bulk.

- We recycled junk. Painting on cereal boxes. (Framing shops often have clearances of card; try carpet shops for samples and wallpaper books from design shops.)

34. Real things

We inherited a nursery bulging with plastic resources. We tried hard to turn this around.

Using real things

We always gave parents a list of things we wanted.

- We used china mugs and plates. We taught the use of real crockery and the children were very good with the china. They were always given the responsibility of stacking the dishwasher. Generally, it would be the same child that had the accidents, however, it was always fascinating to watch a child's face if they had never seen a plate smash before.

- Growing your own fruit, herbs, and vegetables.

- Children had wooden mortar and pestles, and small glass jars for mixing potions. They used real or dried herbs and spices.

- The children used safety knives to chop their own fruit, cheese, and vegetables on chopping boards for their snacks or cooking.

- Children could source their own equipment to cook whenever they wanted to.

- The water tray was equipped with different kinds of brass or metal containers for pouring and measuring.

- Weighing and measuring was also sourced by real things, e.g. conkers, pasta, and rice.

- The nursery had a permanent nature table that could be used as a teaching resource, changing with the seasons. Again, this could be freely and easily changed.

35. The nature table

What can I put on the nature table?

A short autumnal walk will provide you with the following: Conkers – please include their shells, prickly cased sweet chestnuts, acorns, leaves of various colours, blackberries, (cut a small branch and put it into water) wheat, barley, dried grasses, squashes, pumpkins, feathers, animal skeletons owl pellets.

Make sure your table includes hand lenses, kaleidoscopes and books to develop interests.

36. Practical ideas

Hand wash and slippers

We bought in antibacterial handwash for the children; this made an enormous difference. Handwashing was taught and supervised. This, and a combination of outdoor learning, had a positive impact on health.

We also found the children were much calmer wearing slippers in the nursery. It also helped them to become more independent. Every child could manage to put on their own slippers, freeing up time that staff would have used tying laces, etc.

Wellington boots

All children had a pair of boots in nursery; in the summer they also had a sensible pair of outdoor shoes.

Waterproofs

The nursery provided the children with waterproofs.

These were dungarees and jackets, however, in hindsight legs and jackets would have been a better option.

37. Outdoors

Our nursery garden

We hoped that every child would be electric with thrilldom in our nursery garden.

Our nursery garden was a treasure of discoveries, imaginary play, exploration, nature, and science. We were lucky enough to have a big space that allowed for climbing, crouching, rolling, mixing, talking, music, songs, forest school activities, painting and building.

Our outdoor learning environment was a risk-assessed environment that allowed children to be safe to do, rather than safe from doing. If children are exposed to risks, they learn to manage their own risks. As indoors the adult role is to facilitate the child's learning, for example, showing den-building techniques.

Spontaneous learning was the key. Children could count, make up songs, become environmentally aware, measure, experience flow, gravity, and forces. They were appropriately dressed for the different weather. Open-ended resources, such as blocks, offer a vast range of experiences enriching every area of the curriculum and supporting child development. Because blocks are so versatile, they offer endless opportunities for the child's imagination while discovering mathematical and scientific principles, practising problem-solving techniques and social skills, and building a solid foundation for future education.

Learning through play the children could problem-solve, recall, investigate and question. While being outside the children developed their own stories, took photographs, explored art, researched, and enquired.

In Dr Samuel Dennis's study of natural classrooms (2014) he notes that children in outdoor classrooms find their play to be supported both through the natural and structural environment. He states: "Nature provided far more play props and open-ended play opportunities that sites with fixed equipment set in large areas of safety surfacing." Dennis concludes: "Children in natural settings were reported to be more relaxed, focused, engaged, cooperative, creative, nurturing, and happy compared to children in indoor classrooms or in traditional playgrounds."

Nature-based early childhood learning environments provided opportunities for children to experience the changing seasons and observe the life cycle of plants, animals, and insects, while providing natural materials for exploration and play.

Pippa is a prime example of a child who found what she needed in the nursery garden – her choice was swinging. She became our resident bat. We knew that swinging is a sensory experience that helps the brain to acquire the necessary skills to respond to movement and gravity. She didn't, but she found it enjoyable, satisfying and fun.

No matter how much research we read, or how much science behind everything we do, play is the key. It is never a revelation that this unique ingredient underlies all good practice.

Forest School

What is a forest school?

Forest school works with children outdoors over a period of time, introducing responsible risk-taking and setting children up to achieve. Children are supported in their learning and encouraged to explore the outdoor environment and to appreciate nature.

Forest school leaders use learning and teaching strategies, which develop confidence, emotional resilience, independence, language, and communication skills and increase levels of physical activity and mental well-being.

Why do forest schools?

Forest school is a philosophy to equip children with an education that encourages an appreciation of the natural world. Children are encouraged to be independent and by working on small achievable tasks in a stimulating environment they are able to build their own self-esteem and develop social and behavioural management skills.

How and what?

- Nursery should provide waterproof clothing.
- Each child will need to leave their own pair of wellington boots in nursery.
- During hot weather, each child must be protected with sun cream, long sleeves, and a sun hat.

THERE IS NO SUCH THING AS INAPPROPRIATE WEATHER, ONLY INAPPROPRIATE CLOTHING

- Over the year the nursery can follow the changing seasons; trees, sticks, leaves, birds, bugs, new life, and growth.
- Den building, tool work and knot tying are regular activities that will take place throughout the year.
- Children and adults will respect the environment and from day one we will respect the fact that we do not enter the fire pit.
- The programme of fire safety will be introduced followed by a programme of fire-lighting and cooking.

Being safe

Safety at forest school is the vital key. Detailed risk assessment must be standard practice. All staff, children are made fully aware of each part of the risk assessments.

Forest school trained staff and a first aider are always present.

38. REAL and REAL maths

REAL – Raising Early Achievement in Literacy

> "If you want your child to be intelligent, read them fairy tales. If you want them to be more intelligent, read them more fairy tales."
> Albert Einstein

Engaging parents in their children's early literacy development has been shown to improve children's outcomes and help to narrow the gap between disadvantaged and other children.

Making it REAL (Raising Early Achievement in Literacy) is used in the nursery. A series of planned events happen each term. These may include visitors, themed days and visits that work to support children's early literacy and development.

The practitioner builds parents' knowledge and confidence so that they can help their children with reading and writing and create an early home-learning environment.

Home visits to some children are undertaken.

What is the REAL approach?

Making it REAL draws evidence from the original REAL project delivered by Professors Cathy Nutbrown and Peter Hannon at the University of Sheffield.

REAL uses a framework called 'ORIM' (Opportunities, Recognition, Interaction and Model), which is based on the idea that there are four main ways in which parents can help their children's literacy development.

The teacher shares ORIM with families through a series of home visits and literary events. This helps and encourages the family in supporting their child's early literacy.

Our REAL Journey

Like everything that is a new initiative, REAL needs commitment from any practitioner and REAL training is essential.

Literacy is one of the most important areas of learning in the Early Years and working with families has to be a high priority. We wanted to provide something that would make a significant difference.

REAL training was delivered to staff, parents were invited to a presentation, events were delivered, and home visits happened.

The ideas for events is endless, ours included a book camp, a visit to Waterstones bookshop, a mums' mark-making morning. Befriend your local librarian they are a goldmine.

We introduced a daily book-share, which involved parents and staff sharing books with the children every day.

Each year new events were added to the existing ones.

We also began to deliver REAL maths alongside our REAL.

However, with the constraints of staffing it was impossible to deliver home visits for both maths and literacy.

We were fortunate to be able to purchase home reading packs. These are sent home on a weekly basis to all the children, enabling them to share books with their families.

We gradually began to expand REAL throughout the early years, with Reception and Year 1 implementing it.

Flexibility and adaptability are key. The activities need to suit the needs and interests of the individual child. Where it was impossible to undertake a home visit, we found a quiet place in school to deliver the content.

A small pack of pencils, colours, scissors, paper and a Pritt stick are a useful gift to ensure activities can be followed on at home. The National Children's Bureau produces four booklets for parents. These cover the four different strands of REAL – oral language, books, environmental print, and writing.

39. Final words

It would be wonderful if each and every child could have all of these experiences.

It is always a joy to see children with deep involvement and well-being. Their confidence, creativity and levels of learning growing in a secure, happy, organized environment.

Don't be fooled, it does not happen overnight, and it is not easy. It takes a big effort to keep juggling all the balls in the air, and you will come across resistance from staff and senior management. They may not have a full or broad understanding of how the Early Years works or how young children learn. Often, they are driven by a political agenda and this may include financial restrictions and a need for tight assessment.

You will find that once you take the big first step things will roll. It will become easy to build upon measures you have put in place. You can add to resources, finding better ways to tackle problems.

When you see higher levels of engagement, motivation and well-being you will find a reward for your hard work.

It is important to make a difference.

We do not know what the world will be like when these children reach adulthood; what kinds of vocations will be on offer.

The truth is that being self-motivated, sociable, and working with others is the highest priority in any world. We are preparing children to be citizens, so they think for themselves, ask questions and stand up for what they believe.

We want to empower the future generation to shape the world, so we can be happy in the knowledge that the world is indeed in safe hands.

Appendix 1

Beach School Handbook

Contents Of Handbook

1. The Beach School Ethos

2. Our Beach School Code of Conduct

3. Safeguarding Children, Confidentiality and Beach School

4. Equal Opportunities, Inclusion and Beach School

5. Risk Assessment Guidelines

6. Accident and Emergency Procedures

7. Poor Weather Procedures

8. Insurance

9. Beach School Activities

10. Beach School Clothing

11. Environmental Considerations

12. Beach School Handbook for Staff

1. The Beach School Ethos

Beach School is a unique educational experience and process that offers children the opportunity to succeed and develop confidence and self-esteem through hands-on learning experiences in a beach environment.

Children engage in motivating and achieving tasks and activities throughout the year and in all weathers.

Children will play, learn boundaries of behaviour – both physical and social, grow in confidence, self-esteem and motivation while developing an understanding of the natural world.

A Beach School encourages children to:

- develop personal and social skills
- work through practical problems and challenges
- play and create, build, or manage
- discover how they learn best
- pursue knowledge that interests them
- learn how to manage failures
- build confidence in decision making and evaluating risk
- develop practical skills
- understand the benefits of a balanced and healthy lifestyle
- explore connections between humans, wildlife, and the earth
- regularly experience achievement and success
- reflect on learning and experiences
- develop their language and communication skills
- improve physical motor skills
- become more motivated
- improve their concentration skills

2. Our Beach School Code of Conduct

We will be respectful and know that when at the beach specific expectations are in place. We will explore, investigate, learn, and play in a manner that will not damage our environment. We understand that we share the beach with plants and animals.

Lighting a fire

When lighting a fire, the beach school leader will take control of the operation and all accompanying adults will be briefed before we start. A lit fire will not be left unattended at any point. A fire may not be lit until it has been confirmed to all that our fire safety equipment is in place. Open fires will be built within a fire circle.

At the fire circle

An open fire will be lit within a fire circle. A fire circle using log-sitting stools may be established around the perimeter, 1.5m from the fire square. No one may enter the fire circle perimeter unless invited to do so by an adult. There may be no running past the fire circle. No items must be carried and placed within the fire circle unless by an adult. If you wish to move around the fire to a new stool you must step out of the circle and walk around the outside of the log circle. Even when the fire is unlit, we will treat it as if it is lit.

3. Safeguarding Children, Confidentiality and Beach School

Everyone has a responsibility in relation to child protection.

We are committed to:

- Taking all reasonable measures to safeguard and promote the welfare of each child and young person (pupil) in our care.
- The practice of safe recruitment in checking the suitability of staff and volunteers to work with children and young people.
- Protecting each pupil from any form of abuse, whether from an adult or another pupil.

Our aims:

- To raise awareness of individual responsibilities in identifying and reporting cases of abuse.
- To provide a systematic means of monitoring, recording, and reporting of concerns and cases.
- To provide guidance on recognizing and dealing with suspected child abuse.
- To provide a framework for inter-agency communication and effective liaison.
- To ensure that any deficiencies or weaknesses in child protection arrangements are remedied without delay.
- To ensure that safe recruitment procedures are operated.
- To design and operate procedures that promote this policy and which, as far as possible, ensure that teachers and others who are innocent are not prejudiced by false allegations.
- To contribute to the operation of appropriate health and safety procedures
- To have regard to and be consistent with relevant statutory and regulatory requirements and guidance.

In addition, adults working within beach school need to appreciate that when children feel comfortable and content, when their instinct to trust and risk-take is encouraged, they may be moved to disclose information that they might have otherwise kept to themselves. Any volunteer, or member of staff, who finds that a child is telling them something that concerns them should follow the course of action set out below in simple steps:

- Listen to the pupil but ask NO leading questions. Allow the child to lead the discussion but do not press for details.
- Keep calm and offer reassurance. Accept what the child says without challenge.
- Make NO promises. You cannot 'keep a secret'. You should make it understood that there are limits to confidentiality at the start of the disclosure.
- Inform the Head.
- Keep an accurate, written record of the conversation, including the date, the time, the place the conversation occurred in and the essence of what was said and done by whom and in whose presence. Keep the record secure.

4. Equal Opportunities, Inclusion and Beach School

Value is placed on the individuality of all our children. We are committed to giving each child every opportunity to achieve the highest of standards, irrespective of ethnicity, religion, attainment, age, disability, gender or background. We actively seek to remove the barriers to learning and participation that can hinder or exclude individual children or groups of children. We aim to provide all our children with the opportunity to succeed, and to reach the highest level of personal achievement.

We will:

- Ensure equality of access for all children.
- Employ a range of styles, including collaborative learning, so that children can value working together.
- Seek to involve all parents in supporting their child's education.
- Take account of the performance of all children when planning for future learning and setting challenging targets.
- Make best use of all available resources to support the learning of all groups of children.

We ensure that our children:

- Feel secure and know that their contributions are valued.
- Appreciate and value the differences in others.
- Take responsibility for their own actions.
- Participate safely, in clothing that is appropriate to their religious beliefs.
- Are taught in groupings that allow them all to experience success.
- Use materials that reflect a range of cultural backgrounds, learning styles and linguistic needs, without stereotyping.
- Have a common curriculum experience that allows for a range of different learning styles.
- Have challenging targets that enable them to succeed.
- Are encouraged to participate fully, regardless of disabilities or medical needs.

Beach School means Beach School FOR ALL. We encourage a level of risk-taking, always under close adult supervision, and actively foster friendships and collaboration between all children and adults. Beach school activities are always designed to produce success and enjoyment, even when this appears to be of a transitory nature. Children with medical needs or disabilities will be helped so that they can take part fully in each beach school session. Those children with challenging behaviour will be risk assessed and may need one-to-one supervision, but their entitlement to participate in beach school remains the same.

5. Risk Assessment Guidelines

A SITE risk assessment is undertaken, and a check is made prior to every beach school session.

In addition, an ACTIVITY risk assessment will be established prior to any activity that may require it. Specific additional risk assessments will be undertaken for children whose medical condition, or whose behaviour, requires them.

- Risk assessment sheets must be completed before each trip.
- Satisfactory precautions need to be in place, so that the risk is small.
- The risk assessment to keep children safe in a marine environment.
- We look for potential hazards.
- Staff are police checked.
- First aider.
- Emergency procedures in place.
- First aid sheet for paramedics – dietary and medical requirements.
- Off-site parental permission forms.
- Correct clothing.
- Reinforce safety routine.
- Pre-site visit. Risk assessment forms to be completed.
- Beach school rucksack.
- Correct staff ratio: 3–5 years 1 adult/4.

We decide who might be at harm.

- We think about how harm may occur and the worst outcome that we could face.
- We evaluate the current level of risk.
- We decide on a course of action or set of precautions that will be put in place to minimize the potential risk.

We then re-evaluate the level of risk once our course of action and precautions have been put in place.

6. Accident and Emergency Procedures

- Procedures should already be in place for this.
- Call emergency services.
- Notify the school – they will notify the parents.
- Have all medical details to hand.
- Fill out accident report on return.
- Follow up.

Missing Child

- Same procedure as above but commence search immediately.

7. Poor Weather Procedures

We will not go to Beach School if the conditions are deemed dangerous, such as in high winds, during thunderstorms, or during periods of extreme cold. We will use the UK met office online forecast to make judgements about the expected conditions.

A copy of tide times and the weather forecast must be printed out for trip.

Rucksack

Beach school rucksack must be taken.

8. Insurance

All States of Jersey Schools are covered by the same insurance policy. This allows children to undertake beach school activities.

9. Beach School Activities

- Sun dial clocks.
- Shapes of stones.
- Compasses.
- Maps and hidden numbers.
- Tubes floating codes.
- Metal detectors.
- Skeleton making.
- Frame with fingers.
- Rock pooling.
- Beach in a jar.
- City with volcano.
- Pebble sculptures.
- Mosaic pictures.
- Sand art.
- Soap boats.
- Collecting.
- Shipwreck – tarp – quarters.
- Dam building.
- Windsocks.
- Make bling.
- Beach crowns.
- Target with bull's eye.
- Sticks.

10. Beach School Clothing

- Layered clothing.
- Extra thick socks, hat, gloves.
- Wellington boots at all times of the year.
- Always long trousers and long sleeves.
- Waterproof dungarees and jackets(children).
- Waterproofs (adults).
- Sunhat and sun cream in the summer months.
- Named change of clothing in a named rucksack to be left in minibus.

11. Environmental Considerations

- Our beach school activities must be viewed as one with the environment.
- We must make the children aware of the holistic nature of the environment and the impact of human activity.
- Develop an awareness of the environment.
- Children are taught to respect their environment.
- Look for practical ways we can help the environment, e.g. pick up litter.
- Becoming involved in a conservation project.
- Leaving the beach as we have found it.
- Turning stones back over in rock pools.
- Use a range of venues. This will improve the quality of learning.
- Leave attached seaweed in place.

12. Beach School Handbook for Staff

- Policy and procedures to keep children safe in a marine environment
- Requirements:
- Correct staff/child ratio.
- Staff police checked.
- Pre-site visit.
- First aider.
- Beach school rucksack (see attached list of contents).
- Contact details.
- Emergency procedure.
- First aid sheet for paramedics – dietary requirements or medical requirements.
- Off-site parental permission forms.
- Make sure each child has correct clothing and equipment.
- Reinforce safety routine.

Risk assessment.

- Risk assessment to be undertaken before each trip.
- Sheet must be completed, and pre-site visit undertaken.
- Satisfactory precautions need to take place, so that the risk is small.

Weather forecast and tide times

These must be printed out.

Rucksack

Rucksack Contents List:
- First aid kit.
- Medical details.
- Contact details.
- Pen and paper.
- Medication.
- Whistle.
- Mobile phone.
- Change for payphone.
- Children's spare clothes.
- Adult's spare clothes.
- Spare socks and gloves – adult's and children's.
- Water.
- Carrier bags.
- Tissues and toilet paper.
- Wet wipes.
- Foil blankets.
- Survival bag.
- Small sleeping bag.
- Bothy.
- Camera.
- Throw line.

Appendix 2

Forest School Handbook

School Nursery Forest School Handbook

We used this handbook as a guide to our activities in the nursery garden as they included forest school activities too.

Obviously, this handbook will need to be adapted to suit your situation. Our garden was on the school site, so we took that into consideration.

Contents of Handbook

The Forest School Ethos.

Our Forest School Code of Conduct.

Suggested Activities for Forest Schools.

Equipment for Forest School.

Using and Storing Tools.

Health and Safety Policies.

Equal Opportunities, Inclusion and Forest School.

Risk Assessment Guidelines.

1. The Forest School Ethos

Forest School is a unique educational experience and process that offers children the opportunity to succeed and develop confidence and self-esteem through hands-on learning experiences in our garden environment.

Children engage in motivating and achieving tasks and activities throughout the year and in all weathers. Children will work with tools, play, learn boundaries of behaviour – both physical and social, grow in confidence, self-esteem and motivation and develop an understanding of the natural world.

A forest school encourages children to:

- develop personal and social skills
- work through practical problems and challenges
- use tools to create, build or manage
- discover how they learn best
- pursue knowledge that interests them
- learn how to manage failures
- build confidence in decision making and evaluating risk
- develop practical skills
- understand the benefits of a balanced and healthy lifestyle
- explore connections between humans, wildlife and the earth
- regularly experience achievement and success
- reflect on learning and experiences
- develop their language and communication skills
- improve physical motor skills
- become more motivated
- improve their concentration skills

2. Our Forest School Code of Conduct

Entering the garden

We will enter the garden with respect. We will explore, investigate, learn and play in a manner that will not damage our environment. We understand that we share our garden with plants and animals.

Boundaries

Children are made aware of how far they can explore and of any fixed boundary markers. If children move to explore hidden areas an adult should also move into the cover deep enough to be able to see the children but allowing the children the freedom to explore independently.

Lighting a fire

The children will be taught about the garden fire circle. This is an area that is never entered except by invitation of an adult. When children have learnt this rule, then fires may be lit.

When lighting a fire, the forest school leader will take control of the operation and all accompanying adults will be briefed. A lit fire will not be left unattended at any point. A fire may not be lit until it has been confirmed to all that our fire safety equipment is in place.

An open fire will be lit within the fire circle. A fire circle, is made using sitting stools around the perimeter, 1.5m from the fire. No one may enter the fire circle perimeter unless invited to do so by an adult. There may be no running past the fire circle. No items must be carried and placed within the fire circle unless by an adult. If you wish to move around the fire to a new stool you must step out of the circle and walk around the outside of the log circle. Even when the fire is unlit we will treat it as if it is lit.

Using tools

All tools have their own clear code of conduct for correct use, which will include consideration of specific personal protective equipment, correct use of a specific body posture, and consideration of the appropriate types of activity that each tool may be used for.

Picking up and playing with sticks

Children can carry sticks shorter than their arm's length but are encouraged to think about how close they are to other children. Longer sticks may be dragged or carried with the help of another person when each person is at either end. Sticks must not be thrown. Sticks must not be pulled from living trees.

Collecting wood

Wood is collected for fire lighting purposes. It is collected in four thicknesses – matchstick sized, pencil sized, thumb sized and wrist sized. This is a good mathematical activity involving sorting and matching. Sticks may be collected for creating pictures and patterns but should be collected sparingly so as not to disrupt creature habitats.

Leaving the site

- We make sure that the site is left how we found it. We tidy and clear away any trace that we have been there.
- Shelters can be left up, depending on the weather.
- All rubbish and toileting items will always be removed.
- If artefacts have been found or made these may be taken off the site with the consent of an adult.

3. Suggested Activities for Forest Schools

Activities for Forest Schools are diverse and numerous, but it should be remembered that we are trying to create independent learners who are inspired to try out their own ideas, explore their own interests and to attempt new ideas.

Some activities might include:

- Shelter building.
- Fire lighting.
- Tool use.
- Studying wildlife.
- Sensory activities.
- Cooking on an open fire.
- Using a Kelly Kettle.
- Rope and string work.
- Art and sculpture work.
- Developing stories and drama, and meeting imaginary characters.

4. Equipment for Forest School

In addition to tools suited to the planned-for activities, the garden trolley will always be taken.

Trolley contents

The contents of the trolley will vary depending on the time of year and weather conditions, and the planned for activities according to the relevant risk assessments and daily risk assessment. There are of course also essential items that should be carried out for every session.

Essential equipment:

- First aid kit (see contents list, contents review record).
- Emergency procedures.
- Medical information for each individual and emergency contact details.
- Risk assessments.
- Communication device – mobile phone. (Our mobile phone was called Caroline, thanks to a generous donation by a parent.)
- Clean Water.
- Medication for individuals.
- Appropriate clothing.
- Sharps box and gloves.
- Wet wipes, hand gel, nappy sacks, black sacks, towel, water, clothing list.

First aid kit

- Contact cards (location using postcode and OS grid reference)
- Latex Gloves
- Bandages
- Plasters
- Burns gel
- Burn dressing
- Dressings
- Eye wash
- Scissors
- Water
- Sterile water
- Bites and stings cream
- Essential equipment when having a fire
- Flame retardant gauntlet gloves
- Bucket of water
- Fire steel

5. Using and Storing Tools

All tools are counted out and back in at the beginning and end of each session in which they are used. When not in use in the forest they are kept secured away in a locked shed. Before each tool is to be used it will be checked for damage and working order.

Tools are only used for a specific purpose. All adults should model correct and safe tool use, storage and transportation at all times.

Potato peelers and knives – for peeling or sharpening sticks (whittling).

A ratio of 1 adult to 2 children will be observed. This tool must be used seated on a log with elbows placed upon knees and using the tool in a downward motion between the legs.

Kelly Kettle

The forest leader may use this to heat water. Never leave the bung in while heating water. This is only to be in place during storage so as to keep the chamber clear from debris or insects and minibeasts. Once the fire is going in the Kelly Kettle base carefully add the chimney top to it by holding the handle parallel to the ground, and supported on each side by your hands. When lit, do not stand directly over, or look straight down, the chimney. Never blow into the top. When pouring out the water support the base by holding the bung chain in one hand and the handle with the other. To put the fire out, pour the remaining water into the base.

6. Health and Safety Policies

The trained and named Forest School Leader is always the person in charge of forest school sessions.

The Forest School Leader has overall duty of care for the children in their charge. However, all adults involved in the forest school session are required to take all reasonable steps to ensure that children are safe.

The Forest School Leader will review the risk assessments.

7. Equal Opportunities, Inclusion and Forest School

We are committed to giving each child every opportunity to achieve the highest of standards, irrespective of ethnicity, religion, attainment, age, disability, gender or background. We actively seek to remove the barriers to learning and participation that can hinder or exclude individual children or groups of children. We aim to provide all our children with the opportunity to succeed, and to reach the highest level of personal achievement.

We will:

- Ensure equality of access for all children.
- Employ a range of styles, including collaborative learning, so that children can value working together.
- Seek to involve all parents in supporting their child's education.
- Take account of the performance of all children when planning for future learning and setting challenging targets.
- Make best use of all available resources to support the learning of all groups of children.
- Our teachers ensure that our children:
- Feel secure and know that their contributions are valued.
- Appreciate and value the differences in others.
- Take responsibility for their own actions.
- Participate safely, are taught in groupings that allow them all to experience success.
- Use materials that reflect a range of cultural backgrounds, learning styles and linguistic needs, without stereotyping.
- Have a common curriculum experience that allows for a range of different learning styles.
- Have challenging targets that enable them to succeed.
- Are encouraged to participate fully, regardless of disabilities or medical needs.

8. Risk Assessment Guidelines

A SITE risk assessment is undertaken each week and a DAILY risk assessment and check is made prior to sessions in our garden site.

In addition, an ACTIVITY risk assessment will be established prior to any activity that may require it. These will include: whittling, cutting wood, shelter building, fire lighting and cooking on an open fire.

Specific additional risk assessments will be undertaken for children whose medical condition or whose behaviour requires them.

The risk assessment process is detailed below:

- We look for potential hazards.
- We decide who might be at harm.
- We think about how harm may occur and the worst outcome that we could face.
- We evaluate the current level of risk.
- We decide on a course of action or set of precautions that will be put in place to minimise the potential risk.
- We then re-evaluate the level of risk once our course of action and precautions have been put in place.
- We regularly monitor and review each risk assessment, as an action is needed.

Appendix 3

Risk Assessment Template

Nursery Garden Risk Assessment

- Please note a first aid kit and first aider are always on site.
- No forest school activities are undertaken without a trained forest schooler on site.
- Hand washing facilities are always available. Hand washing on return to Nursery.
- Children are always appropriately dressed with correct footwear.
- Children are given clear guidelines and boundaries.
- Children are taught safety outside.
- Weather checked every morning for Jersey forecast.

Hazard	What might happen?	Who is at risk?	How risky is it?	What should be done?
Fire	Burns	All		1:2 ratio. Fire blankets ready. First aider on site. Marked exclusion zone. Staff Forest School trained/Guider training. Kelly Kettle on slab to keep it even. Training given to all. Fire gloves.
Slips, trips and falls.		All		Staff and young people to wear appropriate footwear to minimise the risk of slipping or tripping. Young people given clear boundaries as to the area they can access. Trails and paths to be routinely monitored for obstacles or potential dangers such as falling branches.
Insect bites and stings.		All		It is probable that a variety of insects, that can bite or sting, will be around in any woodland environment. • All parents have completed an Essential Information sheet advising of any known allergic reactions to insect bites and stings.
Infection, specifically through consumption.		All		Children/adults must not eat or drink whilst engaged in activities. Children must not eat anything they find in the garden without checking with an adult. Children/adults must wash their hands before consuming any food or drink.
Allergic reaction		All		All parents to have completed an Essential Information sheet advising of any known allergic reactions. Epipens and inhalers to be carried in the first aid kit.
Poor behaviour		Child		Children to be given clear guidelines as to what behaviour is and is not acceptable during each activity. Parents to have completed an Essential Information sheet advising of any specific risk. Activity to be stopped if the behaviour of any child makes it unsafe.
Fire and cooking		All		In the event of fire all group members to remain together and make their way to the emergency assembly point in K.S.1 playground. Clearly defined and marked fire pit area… space free from equipment or undergrowth around the fire area. Have extra water available to put out fire. Have heat proof gloves and fire blanket available. Safety briefing on fire. High staff pupil ratio. Children taught fire precautions and safety.

Appendix 4

Well-being and involvement

Well-being

Well-being focuses on the extent to which pupils feel at ease, act spontaneously, show vitality and self-confidence. It is a crucial component of emotional intelligence and good mental health. Well-being is also, liked to self-confidence, a good degree of self-esteem and resilience.

The Leuven Scale for well-being

1) Extremely low.

The child clearly shows signs of discomfort such as crying or screaming. They may look dejected, sad, frightened, or angry. The child does not respond to the environment, avoids contact and is withdrawn. The child may behave aggressively, hurting him/herself or others.

2) Low.

The posture, facial expression and actions indicate that the child does not feel at ease. However, the signals are less explicit than under level 1, or the sense of discomfort is not expressed the whole time.

3) Moderate.

The child has a neutral posture. Facial expression and posture show little or no emotion. There are no signs indicating sadness or pleasure, comfort, or discomfort.

4) High.

The child shows obvious signs of satisfaction (as listed under Level 5). However, these signals are not constantly present with the same intensity.

5) Extremely high.

The child looks happy and cheerful, smiles, cries out with pleasure. They may be lively and full of energy. Actions can be spontaneous and expressive. The child may talk to him/herself, play with sounds, hum, sing. The child appears relaxed and does not show any signs of stress or tension. He/she is open and accessible to the environment. The child expresses self-confidence and self-assurance.

The rationale underlying the focus on these two-process dimensions is that high levels of well-being and involvement lead in the end to high levels of child development and deep level learning. This latter concept is centred around the notion that learning should result in significant changes in a pupil's capacity leading to better outcomes in the way that he or she approaches work, relationships, and life in general.

Level of involvement

Involvement focuses on the extent to which pupils are operating to their full capabilities. In particular, it refers to whether the child is focused, engaged, and interested in various activities. Are children intensely engaged in activities? This is considered to be a necessary condition for deep level learning and development.

The Leuven Scale for Involvement

1) Low activity.

Activity at this level can be simple, stereotypic, repetitive, and passive. The child is absent and displays no energy. There is an absence of cognitive demand. The child characteristically may stare into space. N.B. This may be a sign of inner concentration.

2) A frequently interrupted activity.

The child is engaged in an activity, but half of the observed period includes moments of non-activity, in which the child is not concentrating and is staring into space. There may be frequent interruptions in the child's concentration, but his/her involvement is not enough to return to the activity.

3) Mainly continuous activity.

The child is busy at an activity, but it is at a routine level and the real signals for involvement are missing. There is some progress, but energy is lacking, and concentration is at a routine level. The child can be easily distracted.

4) Continuous activity with intense moments.

The child's activity has intense moments during which activities at Level 3 can come to have special meaning. Level 4 is reserved for the kind of activity seen in those intense moments and can be deduced from the involvement signals. This level of activity is resumed after interruptions. Stimuli, from the surrounding environment, however attractive, cannot seduce the child away from the activity.

5) Sustained intense activity.

The child shows continuous and intense activity revealing the greatest involvement. In the observed period not all the signals for involvement need be there, but the essential ones must be present: concentration, creativity, energy, and persistence. This intensity must be present for all the observation period.

Bel Royal School Nursery Case Study using the Leuven Instruments

Introduction

I first heard Ferre Laevers speak at the Nursery World conference in 2015. I found his talk fascinating and was very enthused on my return to nursery. I gave my staff inset on involvement and well-being. Although we did not do this in a formal way we introduced and implemented a number of ideas, looking carefully at our environment and the characteristics of effective learning, and concentrated on feelings. We wanted to achieve deep-level learning.

How using A process-oriented self-evaluation instrument for care settings, (SICS) and a process orientated monitoring system, (POMS), has enabled provision and experiences to be enhanced and reflective of the children in our setting.

- What we did.
- Group screening/ assessment.
- Team discussion/analysis.
- Action plan.
- Evaluate.

In our second year, we started with our 2017–2018 cohort and then worked with our 2018–2019 cohort.

We started from the child's perspective. This enabled us to see clearly how every child in the setting was doing. We used the idea: Can we tweak our practice to the needs and profiles of each individual child?

We used group screening to assess which children were in need of extra support and looked at the particular needs of each child.

The two cohorts of children differed greatly. In 2017–2018 the group climate was not good, with many individual needs. We undertook 2 x group screenings and six rounds of 10 children, using SICS.

The cohort year 2018–2019 was very different. No great changes were needed to the learning environment. However, in the light of advice and suggestions learnt on courses and through reading books and publications, we constantly reorganized and thought about the learning environment and the adult's role in it.

We worked closely with the families of two individual children that had significant needs. This had a great impact on their well-being.

We involved outside agencies and a family support worker with these families.

How did we improve the learning environment?

Action points and interventions to provide a broad and rich environment.

We looked at our environment. We sorted out and dumped any old equipment and gave away equipment that we no longer used.

We used the mantra LESS IS MORE.

Freedom of choice through continuous provision was highlighted.

We introduced more quiet retreat areas. We also provided more spaces where two children could work quietly together.

Snack was changed to give the children more autonomy. Children were free to help themselves to snack, first having to prepare it themselves.

The 2018 cohort loved babies. We bought more baby clothes and buggies, to help develop this area of play.

We realised 2017–2018 cohort needed to be encouraged in the area of language and communication, as over half the cohort were EAL children. We developed the use of puppets and story scribing. We encouraged the children to act out their stories.

We tied in working with the parents through REAL.

We used activities, points of interest and the organization of our day and environment.

We noticed it took the 2017–2018 cohort at least three quarters of an hour to settle whether they were inside or outside. We worked hard to maximise the time spent either inside or outside. Due to the layout of the nursery we do not have free flow. We changed the timings of the day to extend each session to two hours.

We knew that adult interaction was good. However, we worked on not asking a question as a way into the child's play but used wait, observe and listen.

Most involvement was seen in child-initiated activities.

We changed our display walls, to include a lower wall for the children to use for any work they wanted to put up at a lower level.

Appendix 5

Our favourite books for children

It is important to have high quality picture books, both fiction and non-fiction.

Here are our top twenty essential fiction books.

Jasper's Beanstalk by Nick Butterworth and Mick Inkpen.

Shark in the Park by Nick Sharratt.

Kipper's Toybox by Mick Inkpen.

Monkey Puzzle by Julia Donaldson (author) and Axel Scheffler (illustrator).

The Ravenous Beast by Niamh Sharkey.

Don't Put Your Finger in the Jelly, Nelly! by Nick Sharratt.

Shhh! by Sally Grindley (author) and Peter Utton (illustrator).

So Much by Trish Cooke (author) and Helen Oxenbury (illustrator).

Where The Wild Things Are by Maurice Sendak.

The Tiger Who Came to Tea by Judith Kerr.

The Alfie books by Shirley Hughes.

Owl Babies by Martin Waddell (author) and Patrick Benson (illustrator).

The Very Hungry Caterpillar by Eric Carle.

The Oi Frog! series of books by Kes Gray (author) and Jim Field (illustrator).

Mr. Wolf's Pancakes by Jan Fearnley.

Avocado Baby by John Burningham.

Mister Magnolia by Quentin Blake.

Green Eggs and Ham by Dr Seuss.

That Rabbit Belongs to Emily Brown by Cressida Cowell (author) and Neal Layton (illustrator).

We're Going on a Bear Hunt by Michael Rosen (author) and Helen Oxenbury (illustrator).

Appendix 6

Our top twenty favourite illustrators

Jo Howell

Quentin Blake

Judith Kerr

Oliver Jeffers

Tove Jansson

Dick Bruna

Edward Ardizzone

Alex Scheffler

Nick Sharratt

John Burningham

Eric Carle

Beatrix Potter

Helen Oxenbury

Chris Haughton

E. H. Shepard

Emily Gravett

Mick Inkpen

Shirley Hughes

Lauren Child

Ezra Jack Keats

Appendix 7

Always useful a play dough recipe.

It is vital to make this on a weekly basis and in a big enough quantity. Often children will want to dry their model and take it home.

Playdough

Ingredients

4 cups of water
8 teaspoons of oil
2 cups of salt
4 teaspoons of food colouring
4 cups of flour
8 teaspoons of cream of tartar

Method

- Warm the water and oil.

- Add the salt and food colouring (and glitter or flavouring if using) and stir.

- Add the flour and cream of tartar and mix until if forms a firm dough.

- Leave to cool and store in an airtight container.

Appendix 8

Six steps to conflict resolutions (High scope 2014)

- Approach calmly, stopping any hurtful actions.
- Acknowledge children's feelings.
- Gather information.
- Restate the problem.
- Ask for solutions and choose one.
- Be prepared to follow up.

Appendix 9

> **A helpful quote**
>
> *"Teaching should not be taken to imply a 'top down' or formal way of working. It is a broad term that covers the many ways in which adults help young children to learn. It includes their interactions with children during planned and child-initiated play and activities: communicating and modelling language, showing, explaining, demonstrating, exploring ideas, encouraging, questioning, recalling, providing narrative for what they are doing, facilitating, and setting challenges. It takes account of the equipment adults provide and the attention given to the physical environment, as well as the structure and routines of the day that establish expectations."*
>
> Ofsted September 2015

Author's thanks

A big thank-you to all the children and parents of Bel Royal Nursery. Without you this book would not exist.

To my amazing team in the nursery, I love you all and cannot ever thank-you enough for your support. To Jo, my book buddy – your illustrations are wow. Claire Quenault, what can I say about the quality of my very special nursery officer. Official scooper and confident, Millie Bateup, nursery assistant and child whisperer. Doc, Forest School and scientist supreme. Nanny Blampied, lunch lady extraordinaire. Dianah Le Huray, Gill Trott, Ann Lafromboise for your special needs expertise. Lisa Nerac, fellow Early Years champion. Catherine 'twinkle fingers' Baudains, Mrs Sewing Clarke for all your patience over the years.

Thank you Daisy for the brilliantly enjoyable photo shoot. It is quite amazing the various careers past pupils follow. Sarah Houldcroft, my clever publisher, who has made my dream a reality.

Finally, a big thank-you to my new friends at Rouge Bouillon School, for their patience and kindness to my random, but hopefully good ways.

Suppliers

Amazon (Polygel plates) For monoprinting GELLI

References

Page 9   Elliot W. Eisner, 'The kind of schools we need', *Interchange*, 15 (2), (1984), 1–12.

Page 9   Charles Fowler, 'Why the Arts in Education: Saving our Cultural Future', *NASSP Bulletin*, 73 (519), (1989), 90–95.

Page 60   John Dewey, 'Art as Experience', *The Journal of Philosophy*, 31 (10), (1934), 275.

Page 63   Samuel F. Dennis, Jr., Alexandra Wells and Candace Bishop, 'A Post-Occupancy Study of Nature-Based Outdoor Classrooms in Early Childhood Education', *Children, Youth and Environments*, 24 (2), (2014), 35.

Select Bibliography

Books

Bryce-Clegg, Alistair, *Continuous Provision: The Skills* (London: Bloomsbury, 2015)

Bryce-Clegg, *From Vacant to Engaged* (London: Bloomsbury, 2012)

Ceppi, Giulio and Zini, Michele, (ed.), *Children, Spaces, Relations: Metaproject for an Environment for Young Children* (Emilia: Reggio Children,1998)

Csikszentmihalyi, Mihaly, *Creativity: Flow and the Psychology of Discovery and Invention* (London: Harper Collins, 1996)

Csikszentmihalyi, Mihaly, *Flow: The Psychology of Optimal Experience* (Sydney: Harper Collins, 1990)

Danks, Fiona, Schofield, Jo, Williamson, Pete (illus.), *Wild Things* (London: Lonely Planet Kids, 2019)

Legi Editions, *Development Matters in the Early Years Foundation Stage (EYFS)* (London: Department for Education, 2012)

Dowling, Marion, *Young Children's Personal, Social and Emotional Development* (London: Sage, 2014)

Dowling, Marion, *Young Children's Thinking*, (London: Sage, 2012)

Ephgrave, Anna, *Planning in the Moment with Young Children* (Abingdon: Routledge, 2018)

Fisher, Julie, *Interacting or Interfering?* (Maidenhead: Open University Press, 2016)

Fisher, Julie, *Starting from the Child: Teaching and Learning in the Foundation Stage. Teaching and Learning from 4–8* (Maidenhead: Open University Press, 2013)

Froebel, Friedrich, *The Education of Man* (New York: Dover, 2012)

Hanscom, Angela J., *Balanced and Barefoot* (Oakland, Ca.: Harbinger, 2016)

Howard-Jones, Paul, *Evolution of the Learning Brain* (Abingdon: Routledge, 2018)

Isaacs, Susan, *Childhood and After: Some Essays and Clinical Studies* (London: Routledge, 2013)

Isaacs, Susan, *Intellectual Growth in Young Children* (Abingdon: Routledge and Kegan Paul, 1930)

Isaacs, Susan, *The Nursery Years* (Abingdon: Routledge, 1945)

Kindler, Anna M., *Child Development in Art* (Reston, Va.: National Art Education Association 1997)

Kolbe, Ursula, *It's Not a Bird Yet: The Drama of Drawing* (Byron Bay, NSW: Peppinot Press, 2005)

Koster, Joan Bouza, *Growing Artists: Teaching the Arts to Young Children* (Belmont, Ca.: Wadsworth, 2014)

Kress, Gunther, *Before Writing: Rethinking the Paths to Literacy* (Abingdon: Routledge, 1996)

Laevers, Ferre, *A Process-Oriented Monitoring System for Early Years [POMS]* (Averbode, Be.: CEGO, 2012)

Laevers, Ferre, *Defining and Assessing Quality in Early Childhood Education* (Leuven, Be.: Leuven University Press, 1994)

Laevers, Ferre, *Involvement of Children and Teacher Style: Insights from an International Study Experiential on Education* (Leuven, Be.: Leuven University Press, 2004)

Laevers, Ferre, *My Profile-Sharing Observations with Parents in the Early Years* (Averbode, Be.: CEGO, 2012)

Laevers, Ferre, *Observing Involvement in Children from Birth to 6 Years: a DVD Training Pack* (Averbode, Be.: CEGO, 2010)

Laevers, Ferre, The Leuven Involvement Scale for Young Children, (Manual and Video), Experiential Education Series, No 1. (Leuven, Be.: Centre for Experiential Education, 1994)

Logan, Jason, *Make Ink* (New York: Abrams, 2018)

Louv, Richard, *Last Child in the Woods* (London: Atlantic, 2010)

Castagnetti, Marina, Giudici, Claudia, et al. *Loris Malaguzzi and the Schools of Reggio Emilia* (Abingdon: Routledge, 2016)

McGonigal, Kelly, *The Willpower Instinct: How Self-Control Works, Why It Matters, and What You Can Do to Get More of It* (New York: Avery, 2011)

McMillan, Margaret, *The Nursery School* (London: Forgotten Books, 2012)

Montessori, Maria, *The Absorbent Mind: A Classic an Education and Child Development for Educators and Parents* (New York: Holt, Rinehart & Winston, 1995)

Montessori, Maria, *Dr. Montessori's Own Handbook* (London: Random House, 1988)

Macfarlane, Robert, Morris, Jackie, *The Lost Words* (London: Hamish Hamilton, 2017)

Nutbrown, Cathy, Hannon, Peter, and Morgan, Anne, *Early Literacy Work with Families* (London: Sage, 2005)

Palmer, Sue, *Toxic Childhood* (London: Orion, 2015)

Parker-Rees, Rod, (ed.), Willan, Jenny, (ed.), *Early Years Education* (*Major Themes in Education*), (Abingdon: Routledge, 2005)

Piaget, Jean, *To Understand is to Invent* (London: Penguin, 1977)

Read, Herbert, *Education Through Art* (London: Faber and Faber, 1961)

Rogers, Carl R., *On Becoming a Person* (London: Constable and Robinson, 2004)

Stewart, Nancy, *How Children Learn*. St Albans: Early Education, 201)

Tassoni, Penny, *Reducing Educational Disadvantage: A Strategic Approach in the Early Years* (London: Bloomsbury, 2016)

Vecchi, Vea, *Art and Creativity in Reggio Emilia: Exploring the Role and Potential of Ateliers in Early Childhood Education (Contesting Early Childhood)* (Abingdon: Routledge, 2010)

Vygotski, L. S. *Mind In Society: Development of Higher Psychological Processes* (Cambridge, Ma.: Harvard University Press,1978)

Wright, S. (ed.), *The Arts in Early Childhood* (Parkside, ADEL: Prentice Hall, 1997)

Journals

Georgina Barton, 'Arts-based Educational Research in the Early Years' *International Research in Early Childhood Education*, 6 (1), (2015), 62–78.

A. Davis, and Cathy Nutbrown, 'Threads of Thinking', *The British Journal of Educational Studies*, 43 (1), (1995), 98.

Samuel F. Dennis, Jr., Alexandra Wells, Candace Bishop, 'A Post-occupancy Study of Nature-Based Outdoor Classrooms in Early Childhood Education' *Children, Youth and Environments*, 24 (2), 35.

John Dewey, 'Art as Experience', *The Journal of Philosophy*, 31(10), (1934) 275.

Charles Fowler, 'Why the Arts in Education: Saving Our Cultural Future' *NASSP Bulletin*, 73 (519), (1989), 90–95.

Elliot W. Eisner, 'The Kind of Schools We Need' *Interchange*, 15 (2), (1984), 1–12.

Steven J. Howard, et al, 'Measuring interactional quality in pre-school settings: introduction and validation of the Sustained Shared Thinking and Emotional Wellbeing (SSTEW) scale' *Early Child Development and Care*, 190 (7), 1017–1030.

Ferre Laevers, 'Forward to Basics! Deep Level Learning and the Experiential Approach', *Early Years*, 20 (2), (2000), 20–29.

Ferre Laevers, Bart Declercq, 'How well-being and involvement fit into the commitment to children's rights', *European Journal of Education*, 53 (3), (2018), 325–35.

Cathy Nutbrown, 'Susan Isaacs: A Life Freeing the Minds of Children' *Children & Society*, 25 (3), (2011), 251.

Michael J. Parsons, Anna M. Kindler, 'Child Development in Art' *Studies in Art Education*, 40 (1), (1998), 80.

Iram Siraj-Blatchford, 'Educational disadvantage in the early years: How do we overcome it? Some lessons from research' *European Early Childhood Education Research Journal*, 12 (2), (2004), 5–20.

Edward Scott, 'The Influence of Nursery School Experience in Social Value Acquisition' *Educational Review*, 21 (3) (1969), 226–33.

Bernadet Tijnagel-Schoenaker, 'The Reggio Emilia Approach ... The Hundred Languages' *Prima Educatione*, 1, (2017), 139.

Jef J. van Kuyk, 'Scaffolding – how to increase development?' *European Early Childhood Education Research Journal*, 19 (1) (2011), 133–46.

Marilyn Zurmuehlen, Viktor Lowenfeld, W. Brittain, 'Creative and Mental Growth' *Art Education*, 23 (9), (1970), 45.

Useful websites

Autism Education Trust. *Early Years Resources*. <https://www.autismeducationtrust.org.uk/resources/early-years-resources/> [Accessed 11 September 2020].

Cbeebies – BBC *Games or Kids and Early Years Activities* <https://www.bbc.co.uk/cbeebies> [Accessed 11 September 2020].

Best Start Partnership Jersey. *Best Start Partnership, Jersey Channel Islands*. <https://beststart.je/> [Accessed 11 September 2020].

The Children's Society. *Good Childhood Report 2020*. <https://www.childrenssociety.org.uk/good-childhood-report-2020> [Accessed 11 September 2020].

Comic Relief. *A Just World Free from Poverty* <https://www.comicrelief.com/> [Accessed 11 September 2020].

Early Education. *Home | Early Education*. <https://www.early-education.org.uk> [Accessed 11 September 2020].

Early Excellence. *Early Years Resources, Furniture and Training, Nursery, Infant and Primary School – Early Excellence*. <https://earlyexcellence.com/> [Accessed 11 September 2020].

HighScope. *High-Quality Early Childhood Education* <https://highscope.org/> [Accessed 11 September 2020].

GOV.UK <https://www.gov.uk/government> [Accessed 11 September 2020].

Hungry Little Minds Campaign. *Hungry Little Minds*. <https://hungrylittleminds.campaign.gov.uk/> [Accessed 11 September 2020].

National Literacy Trust. *National Literacy Trust*. <https://literacytrust.org.uk/> [Accessed 11 September 2020].

NCB. *Home*. <https://www.ncb.org.uk/> [Accessed 11 September 2020].

NSPCC Learning. *NSPCC Learning Home.*: <https://learning.nspcc.org.uk/> [Accessed 11 September 2020].

Nursery World. *Nursery World*. <https://www.nurseryworld.co.uk/> [Accessed 11 September 2020].

Research Gate. *Taking Play More Seriously*. <https://www.researchgate.net/publication/283149621_Taking_play_more_seriously_A_Montessori_approach_to_understanding_Free_Flow_Play> [Accessed 11 September 2020].

The University of Sheffield. *Early Childhood / School of Education / The University of Sheffield* <https://www.sheffield.ac.uk/education/research/early-childhood> [Accessed 11 September 2020].

Unicef. *Learning Through Play*. <https://www.unicef.org/sites/default/files/2018-12/UNICEF-Lego-Foundation-Learning-through-Play.pdf> [Accessed 11 September 2020].

Yoga Journal. *Yoga Poses, Meditations, Sequences, and Free Classes*. <https://www.yogajournal.com/> [Accessed 11 September 2020].

PROD. MRS HOWELL
DIRECTOR
CAMERAMAN DAISY
SLATE
TAKE 42!
DATE TODAY!

Printed in Great Britain
by Amazon